11/92

PRESENTING

Zibby Oneal

Twayne's United States Authors Series
Young Adult Authors

Patricia J. Campbell, General Editor

The Young Adult Authors books seek to meet the
need for critical studies of fiction for young adults.
Each volume examines the life and work of one
author, helping both teachers and readers of young
adult literature to understand better the writers they
have read with such pleasure and fascination.

PRESENTING

Zibby Oneal

Susan P. Bloom
Cathryn M. Mercier

Twayne Publishers • Boston
A Division of G. K. Hall & Co.

Presenting Zibby Oneal
Susan P. Bloom and Cathryn M. Mercier

Copyright 1991 by G. K. Hall & Co.
All rights reserved.
Published by Twayne Publishers
A division of G. K. Hall & Co.
70 Lincoln Street
Boston, Massachusetts 02111

Copyediting supervised by Barbara Sutton.
Book production by Janet Z. Reynolds.
Typeset by Compset, Inc., Beverly, Massachusetts.

10 9 8 7 6 5 4 3 2 1

The paper used in this publication meets the minimum requirements
of American National Standard for Information Sciences—Permanence
of Paper for Printed Library Materials, ANSI Z39.48-1984. ∞"

Printed and bound in the United States of America.

Library of Congress Cataloging-in-Publication Data

Bloom, Susan P.
    Presenting Zibby Oneal / Susan P. Bloom, Cathryn M. Mercier.
      p.   cm.—(Twayne's United States authors series ; TUSAS
  585. Young adult authors)
    Includes bibliographical references and index.
    ISBN 0-8057-8216-8
    1. Oneal, Zibby—Criticism and interpretation. 2. Young adult
fiction, American—History and criticism. I. Mercier, Cathryn M.
II. Title. III. Series: Twayne's United States authors series ;
TUSAS 585. IV. Series: Twayne's United States authors series.
Young adult authors.
PS3565.N443Z58   1991
813'.54—dc20   91-11852
                                            CIP

For my mother, Lillian, my husband, David, and my daughter, Johanna.

S.P.B.

For my mother, Elaine.

C.M.M.

Contents

Preface

Zibby Oneal breathes new life into the age-old drama of growing up. Her contemporary realistic novels hold special attraction for a predominantly female, predominantly young adult, audience. With careful psychological completeness, Oneal gives her readers the opportunity to gain insight into themselves by first understanding others. Each of her three young adult characters is a deep, complex girl. Each character behaves nontraditionally within the structure of an otherwise traditional household. Their decent, common households expect them to adopt conventional attitudes and conduct, as do their trouble-free siblings. Unlike the familiar fairy-tale prince whose initiation and coming of age depend on his slaying the dragon and saving the princess and the village, these young women characters are engaged in their own unique dragon slayings. "But who is to say that the dragons encountered are not equally fearsome or that the arrival at the destination has not been just as dearly won?"[1] The girls wage their battles in an intimate psychological landscape where the dragon of growing up demands self-reflection and reevaluation of childhood relationships.

Zibby Oneal's settings, somewhere between the mystical, mythical forests of folktale and the crowded, bustling New York city streets, are the real and imagined islands of today's suburban young people. What is most compelling and resounding about Oneal's books does not reside only in the evocative settings she creates. It is also these interior islands created by the individual children themselves that command attention and memory. Oneal feels "a responsibility to make children understand that adolescence is a self-absorbed world—this may be why I always have islands in my books—but it's not a place you can stay forever. The movement away and out into the world, into concern for other people, has to happen; you aren't adult until you make that move. Sure, explore your feelings . . . but then get into the world."[2]

Carrie, the protagonist of *The Language of Goldfish,* builds both a physical and a psychological island where she seeks to remain sheltered, protected from the intrusions, the difficulties, and the responsibilities of growing up. But denying external realities and the need to grow up prove self-destructive for Carrie. To move beyond despair and desolation, she must discover within herself the dormant capacity to create freely. She must shed the illusion of innocence to embrace fully the pain and the joy of adulthood.

In *A Formal Feeling,* Oneal introduces Anne, a haunted young woman unable to accept her mother's death and her feelings of abandonment because of it. Anne skates, escaping to her own physical island: a patch of ice—forlorn, cold, and remote. On the ice, Anne creates her ideal island: a place untouched by loss or change, a place closed to mourning. She engraves controlled, symmetrical patterns in which she casts memories of a perfect relationship with a perfect mother. With her father's remarriage, Anne must work to see her regal parents in flawed, human terms.

With Kate, the central character of *In Summer Light,* Oneal moves to the very real island of Martha's Vineyard, off the coast of Massachusetts. Like Carrie and Anne, Kate is a uniquely talented adolescent, similarly burdened by the task of growing up. In accepting her own artistic vision, not only must Kate emerge from behind the shadow of her prestigious artist father but also must learn to accept his human frailties.

Whether guised as Carrie, or Anne, or Kate, the child remains the same: struggling to free herself from her illusory fantasies as she begins to emerge from her chrysalis-island and accept her own decent, common realities. This, after all, is the task of every child.

Acknowledgments

We are grateful to Zibby Oneal for her generosity and support as we worked on this book. She kindly provided the photographs of herself and her family included herein. We could count on her to be gracious and fully responsive whenever we picked up the telephone or wrote her a note.

We are indebted to the staff of the Kerlan Collection at the University of Minnesota in Minneapolis, especially Deidre Johnson, for their time, effort, and expediency in providing us with duplicates of the holographs and manuscripts of Zibby Oneal's three young adult novels.

We thank Jazan Higgins and Viking Press for their ongoing investment in the Simmons College Center for the Study of Children's Literature. In providing us copies of Oneal's books upon publication, they have nurtured our interest in the author and her works. Deborah Brodie, Oneal's editor at Viking, gave us invaluable assistance and insight.

This book would not have been possible without Carolyn Shute, whose steady help and cheerful nature make coming to work pleasurable. A pat on the back goes to Adria Deasy for her reliable office assistance.

The moral and financial support of the Simmons College Fund for Research provided us with additional encouragement to pursue this project.

Patty Campbell's reflective questions and comments shaped our final manuscript, and for this we are especially grateful. Thanks are also due to our editors at Twayne: Athenaide Dallett, Liz Fowler, and Carol Chin.

We offer our appreciation to Laura McCollum, for her superb, careful, and precise indexing, and to Lillian Johnson, for her close and attentive reading.

Finally, we gratefully acknowledge permission to quote from the following sources:

Poem 341, "After Great Pain," from *The Complete Poems of Emily Dickinson,* edited by Thomas H. Johnson. Copyright 1929 by Martha Dickinson Bianchi. © Renewed 1957 by Mary L. Hampson.

Unpublished manuscript of talk delivered at "Metamorphosis" Summer Symposium in Children's Literature at the Center for the Study of Children's Literature, Simmons College, Boston, in July 1987, used with permission of Zibby Oneal.

Unpublished correspondence between Deborah Brodie, Viking Press, and Zibby Oneal, 25 October 1984 and 26 February 1985.

Selected quotations from *The Language of Goldfish* by Zibby Oneal, © 1980 by Zibby Oneal, reprinted by permission of Viking Penguin, a division of Penguin Books USA Inc. Selected quotations from *A Formal Feeling* by Zibby Oneal, © 1982 by Zibby Oneal, reprinted by permission of Viking Penguin, a division of Penguin Books USA Inc. Selected quotations from *In Summer Light* by Zibby Oneal, © 1985 by Zibby Oneal, reprinted by permission of Viking Penguin, a division of Penguin USA Inc.

Chronology

1986 Receives Boston Globe–Horn Book Award for *In Summer Light.*

1986 *Grandma Moses: Painter of Rural America,* illustrated by Donna Ruff.

1987 Guest instructor during Summer Symposium "Metamorphosis"; special instructor in Children's Literature at the Center for the Study of Children's Literature at Simmons College, Boston.

1990 *A Long Way to Go,* illustrated by Michael Dooling.

1. Sifting through Experience: An Interview

Zibby Oneal spent four weeks at the Center for the Study of Children's Literature at Simmons College in Boston during the summer of 1987. As guest instructor for the symposium/institute "Metamorphosis," she read and discussed with graduate students in children's literature picture books, books for young and intermediate readers, and young adult novels. The thematic concerns of her novels for young adults, her insights as a gifted reader, and her skills as discussion leader marked her as the ideal person to examine literature for children and young adults through the lens of change and transformation.

During that summer, we came to know and respect Zibby Oneal as an individual, a teacher, and a writer. We eagerly welcomed the opportunity to see her again and were grateful when she agreed to meet with us for an interview while she was in Boston in October 1989. In shaping the interview, we sought to gain information about Zibby Oneal as daughter, wife, and mother; to discover her perceptions about her growth as an author; and to get firsthand knowledge about her intentions as a writer. Our hope was that in learning about her, we would attain new insights into the fiction she creates.

Tell us about your family.

I am married and have two children and am, myself, one of two children. My sister is two years younger than I. We grew up on an ordinary residential street in Omaha, Nebraska, which made the fact that our father raised goats in the back yard all the odder. There were usually two or three of them nibbling at the lilac bushes. I hesitate to mention what eventually happened to those goats. My father was, among other things, involved in medical research. Goats are, apparently, good research subjects.

Our mother bore the presence of the goats stoically, just as she bore our father's other projects. While he was inventing his own salad dressing and seeking to patent it, she bore the chaos in the kitchen. When he moved on to painting portraits, she posed for him. She always said that our father made all the decisions in the house except the important ones. "Which were those?" we asked repeatedly, but she wouldn't say. She kept her own counsel.

She was like her father, our grandfather, in that way. He was missing the tip of his index finger. Over and over we asked where it had gone, and his answer was always the same: "If I tell you what happened, will you promise not to ask any more questions about it?" Always, we promised. "All right, then," he'd say, smiling kindly. "It was bitten off." That's all I know about that or ever did know.

Was this an eccentric family? No family seems eccentric, I suspect, when one is living in the midst of it. It's only later, looking back. . . .

"Zibby" seems an unusual name. Where did it come from?

I am the third in a line of Mary Elizabeths. At some point this name was shortened to Zibby, but that happened before I came along. I have a silver baby's cup that belonged to my mother engraved with the nickname. But, so far as I know, I am the only one who carried this silly name into late middle age. On the other hand, it is a name people remember—if they ever learn it.

I remember the name's being the bane of my childhood. Every

September I had to stand up and spell it for every teacher. I longed for a usual name, like Ann.

What sorts of activities did you enjoy as a child?

For a large part of my childhood, I thought that I was not athletic. What I realize now is that I didn't like girls' kinds of sports: roller skating, jumping rope, hopscotch, that kind of thing. I liked climbing trees, playing commandoes (which meant slithering through vacant lots on my belly, head down in case the enemy was anywhere about), riding my bike with my feet on the handlebars, playing mumblety-peg. I did not consider any of these latter "sports," and so I thought I was not athletic. What I see now is that it was not a matter of being athletic at all. It was a matter of being a girl, or at least a girl as that was defined in the late 1940s. For most of my childhood, my model was Tom Sawyer.

Now, I jog (slowly), play tennis (not very competitively), and walk a lot. I never did learn how to do a graceful swan dive, but I bet I could still do a spectacular cannonball.

What about your schooling?

I started first grade at a convent school where the nuns still wore long black habits and veils. I thought they were wonderful and mysterious in those clothes. I can remember deciding that there was no way they could be walking around on ordinary legs like ordinary human beings. To move so smoothly, I thought, they must be coasting on wheels. Eventually I became friendly enough with one of the nuns to ask whether she had legs. She said she had. So then, emboldened, I asked, "Do you also have hair?" I had to take it on faith that she had both because she wasn't inclined to show me.

I loved that school. I loved the whole convent atmosphere. And it seems to me that we learned a tremendous amount there. We were studying French in first grade, for instance. Although I was there only three years, the school made a great impression on me.

I left the convent after third grade because of gas rationing and my sister's dislike for the school. It made no sense to have us in separate schools, I suppose, and in those wartime years when gas was scarce, driving the extra distance from home to school became a problem. Both of us started instead at a day school that was closer to home.

Was that problematic for you?

Yes. I hated it. I didn't want to be there. I wanted to stay right where I had been. And I never again enjoyed school as much as I did those first three years. At the convent, there had been a quiet, orderly atmosphere and an expectation that the students were there to learn. There wasn't any question about that. No excuses.

Is that what your sister objected to?

Yes, exactly what she objected to. And it really frightened her. The nuns frightened her. The whole atmosphere frightened her. She would routinely vomit each morning before she set off to school, and Mother decided enough was enough.

Stories of nuns often portray them as harsh. Your experience doesn't bear that out.

No; they were wonderfully gentle, absolutely devoted to children and to teaching children. That may have been the difference, really. They had nothing else on their minds. They weren't worrying about getting home to take care of a family. They were infinitely patient and very caring.

You have never re-created that experience at all in any of your books.

No. I've thought about it. It is hard to figure out what to do with first, second, and third grade memories, how to transpose them and use the material with older characters; I don't know how the experience would translate. For instance, a high school student in the same environment might feel very restricted and unhappy. Probably I'll some day use this material in flashbacks.

Would you talk about your relationship with your sister a little more?

Well, actually, I'm writing a book about sisters now. I'm trying to remember that relationship. I remember that when she was born, I felt as if I had been displaced in some kind of way. I was two and one-half, and I can remember feeling almost like a balloon that the air had seeped out of when they brought her home. I really couldn't believe that anybody was going to do this to me. But, then, she wasn't an imposing presence at first, and I got used to her and became rather fond of her. Still, I was always, always jealous of her, I think, and still am. I always had a feeling that she could do everything a little better, that everything came more easily to her—none of which is necessarily true, but it was the way I felt. At the same time, I was very, very close to her. We played together constantly. It was "us against them" a lot of the time. I wouldn't have allowed anybody to lay a hand on her or tease her. I was very protective. So it was that kind of relationship. It was both, all the time, which made it bittersweet.

Sounds pretty normal.

Yes, I know it. That is what I'm trying to talk about in this book—a normal relationship, all its facets. That will be the seminal relationship in the book.

Did you and your sister share similar interests? What is she doing now?

She works at the Art Institute in Chicago. She has a background in classical archaeology and in art history, and she is involved with the museum's collection of antiquities. She has always been interested in art, as I have to a lesser degree. In this we were following our father.

He painted for fun, but he did it as he did everything else—very intensely. He painted from Saturday morning right through to Sunday night on the weekends. And he collected paintings back in the days when one could afford to collect. And so my sister and I both developed an interest in art and some knowledge about it. We absorbed this, just being around him.

Was she also painting, or was her interest more of an academic one?

Academic, although she's very talented with her hands. She does beautiful handwork, whereas I have no talent for that sort of thing.

With your family still in Omaha, was it a dramatic move for you to go to college at Stanford, in California?

I wanted to go to Stanford because I'd been in girls' schools all my life. I didn't know much about boys, really, and I wanted a coeducational environment. I wanted a good school, and I preferred the West.

Did your sister also leave home when she went to college?

She went to boarding school. I think she started at boarding school her freshman year. And she was never really home a whole lot after that. Then she went on to college.

And were you living at home when she was boarding?

Yes, for two years. It seems like much longer. It seems as though she wasn't home the whole time I was in high school, but, of course, that's not right. And then she was away at college. And somehow, after that, we really didn't see each other very much. I didn't see her much until after I was married, after she was married. Then we began to become pretty good friends. It seems that period of being apart smoothed the sandpaper between us. And since some of our children are about the same age, we've made it a point to get together in the summers.

When you went to Stanford, did you know you were going to major in English?

Yes. It was really the only subject I was interested in.

Zibby Oneal at nine months.

Zibby Oneal, 18 months, at her grandparents' house.

Zibby Oneal and her sister Karen, ages seven and nine, outside their house in Omaha.

Zibby and Bob Oneal on their wedding day, 1955.

Zibby Oneal reading to her two children, Lisa and Michael, ages four and six, in 1964.

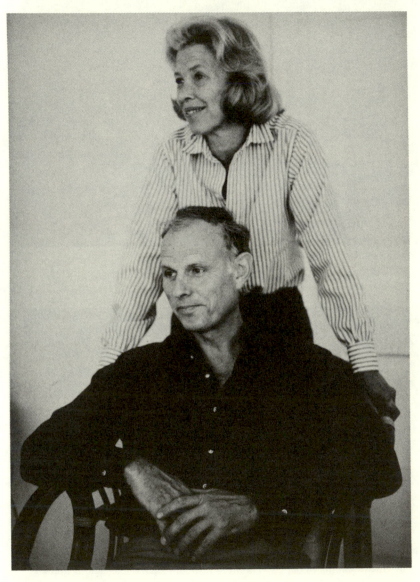

Zibby and Bob Oneal. *Photograph by Stephen Blos.*

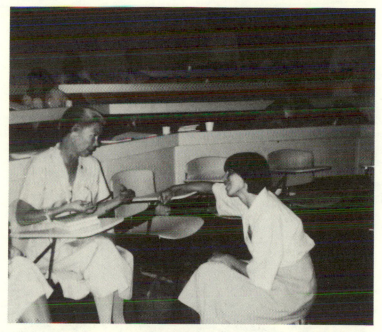

Zibby Oneal at Simmons College "Metamorphosis" institute speaking with Karen Jameyson, former managing editor of the *Horn Book*. *Photograph by Susan P. Bloom.*

Zibby Oneal with Lisa and Michael in Ann Arbor, 1989. *Photograph by Julie Steedman.*

Zibby Oneal. *Photograph by Stephen Blos.*

How long have you been writing?

I began writing when I was very, very young. I made up stories in my head before I could write. It was a way of establishing my own space. From an early age, I would go out and sit under a tree in the back yard and make up stories for myself. It was like moving into another country for a while. Now, in my adult life, when I've not been able to write, when nothing has seemed to work, I've felt that I've lost the passport to that country. That's upsetting.

Talk about your reading background. Were you a reader as a child?

Yes. My mother read to us from as early as I can remember. She was a literary woman herself, and reading was her main delight. She had a good memory for literature. My mother had something like a public library right there at our house. And she had volumes in her head; she would go around quoting. She taught me the "Prologue" to *The Canterbury Tales* before I could read, at three or four years old. On an autumn evening, she would look out the window and quote Keats. And so it was normal for me to think in terms of poetry. When I was being toilet trained, so I am told, my mother discovered me behind the bathroom door muttering, "double, double toidy trouble." Voicing my complaints about the process, I guess, and using the witches' chant from *Macbeth* to do so. At any rate, I had a real appreciation for the sound of language at an early age.

Mother read us all the children's classics, and she kept pace with the new children's books being published, and so we had a very broad background. Later I began reading on my own. I was always reading. I remember the Melendy books in particular. *The Saturdays* was one of the first books I read to myself. At one stage I can remember having a desire to read racy novels—and to do this privately and secretly the way my friends did (my mother wouldn't have objected so I had no real need for secrecy). *Forever Amber* was considered hot stuff in those days, and I bought a copy. One afternoon I had just settled in under my bed with the book on my stomach and a flashlight in hand. I was just approaching one of the "good" parts when the dust ruffle lifted, and there was my mother, looking at me upside down. "If you want to read something really racy," she said, "why don't you try *Ulysses?*" This was my introduction to James Joyce.

But that was her approach: "You want something racy? Why don't you read something racy *and* good?" And by the time I got to high school and college, I was reading with some discrimination.

Did your father engage in this literary banter?

No, not at all. It was as if there were two completely separate lines of influence: the artistic and the literary.

Your sister went one way, and you went the other.

Yes, but there's some crossover. I write about painters and artists, and she does a certain amount of academic writing.

And what do you enjoy reading now?

This is a hard one because I do read so much and enjoy so many, many writers.

There are writers from whom I've learned a lot about writing: Mark Twain, Virginia Woolf, Willa Cather, James Joyce, Thomas Hardy, Jane Austen.

From Twain, Cather, and Hardy, I learned about setting a scene, creating the atmosphere of a place. I've spent a good deal of time studying how they do it—how each one weaves a story, character, and place into a seamless cloth, so that, for instance, the Nebraska prairie is as much a part of *My Ántonia* as is the story of the characters themselves. It is almost as though the characters have grown out of the land in the way the coarse prairie grass has. I'd say the same thing about *Tess of the d'Urbervilles* or *Return of the Native* or *Huckleberry Finn.*

From Joyce and Woolf and Jane Austen, I've learned something about the inner life: how to write about what goes on in a character's head, how to get at and express thoughts and feelings. I suppose it's just about impossible to be writing in the late twentieth century and not be influenced by Joyce, and perhaps also by Woolf—if not directly, then certainly indirectly—just as it is probably impossible not to be influenced by Freud. They've become part of the way we think.

From all these writers, I've learned something about plot. Plot needs to evolve out of character rather than being artificially imposed. Willa Cather says it much better: "After [an author] has once or twice done a story that formed itself, inevitably, in his mind, he will not often turn back to the building of external stories again." When character dictates events, there is a sense of inevitability that is much more satisfying than a prefabricated plot. I think I first began to appreciate this through reading the authors listed above.

Then there are books read in bed or by the fire. Alice Walker, Toni Morrison, Margaret Drabble, Joan Didion, Mary Gordon, Anne Tyler. For about two years, I seemed to read mainly women novelists. I'm not sure whether this represented feminist solidarity on my part or whether I was simply in the mood for a variety of female viewpoints. But I also read anything by E. L. Doctorow, John Updike, Saul Bellow, Philip Roth. I loved *Bonfire of the Vanities.* Lately I've been reading John Casey and William Kennedy.

Sometimes I feel like something old and loved and familiar, and then I tend to read Eudora Welty or Anthony Trollope or Jane Austen or Colette. Often I read mysteries. I especially like Ngaio Marsh and P. D. James.

Because I taught "Great Books" in the freshman honors program for quite a few years, I read things that I would not normally pick off the shelf: Dante's *Divine Comedy,* Thucydides' *History of the Peloponnesian War,* for example. Now that I've read them five or six times, in order to teach them every year, they feel like old friends.

And there are those books that I wish I'd read: *Remembrance of Things Past,* by Marcel Proust; the Bible. I always remember the line from *Goodbye, Columbus,* in which the narrator says he knows it must be summer because his cousin is trying to read *War and Peace* again. I feel like that about Proust and the Bible. Sum-

mer after summer I promise myself that I'll read—finish—one or
the other, but summer after summer I don't. I get started, and
then something happens. It isn't that I don't enjoy what I'm reading, it's just all those pages!

And I have a list of books I would wish to re-read: all the Rus-
sians, a lot of the poetry that I once adored but haven't read in
years, and most of Dickens.

As you can see, I don't read much nonfiction—mainly biographies and not many of those. I did read a biography of the painter
Mary Cassatt recently, written by Nancy Hale, and thought it was
wonderful—everything a biography should be (meaning it read a
lot like fiction).

Do you read young adult novels now?

Some. Not many. They aren't intended for someone my age. That's
one thing. More important, I don't want to know what other writers are doing, at least when I'm in the midst of writing myself.
It's not helpful. It undermines my confidence.

What about your husband's background?

He grew up just outside Chicago and had a normal boy's life:
played football and so on in high school, then went to Dartmouth
and to Harvard Medical School. Eventually he came to Ann Arbor
to do a residency. I met him at a friend's wedding. He was an
usher, and I was a bridesmaid. I was twenty-one when we married. I stopped my work at Stanford in the middle of my junior
year and didn't finish a degree until ten years later, at the University of Michigan, after the children were in school.

*What prompted you to go back to school? Did you always know
you would?*

I wouldn't have stopped when I did except that we were at opposite ends of the country and there was no way to commute, really.
And I thought, well, I could go back to school in Boston, while he's
at Harvard. But, of course, then we found that I had to work. I

had to support us, and I didn't have time to do both. I did take some courses at Boston University at night. Then we had the children. As soon as they were in school, I went back and finished.

What kind of work did you do while your husband was in school?

I worked for two obstetricians first, as a secretary. They were just getting started, and they didn't have very many patients, so I could handle them both. When we moved to Michigan, I worked for the university's philosophy department, again as a secretary, until Lisa was born. Two years later, my son was born.

Both children live in New York now. Michael is an editor at *Business Week*. Lisa is a social worker at a school for learning-disabled children. She's married. He isn't.

Do you look forward to being a grandmother?

I'll say I do. I have already knitted a blanket, although there are no prospects on the horizon at the moment. My thought was that since I knit so slowly, I ought to get started well ahead.

If you were to do it over again, would you have married as early?

Absolutely not. One of my great regrets is that I didn't spend some time on my own: working, living on my own, maybe getting a graduate degree, certainly finishing college. No, I'd never do it that way again. It's ridiculous to marry when you're twenty-one. You're a baby.

How has being a doctor's wife affected your life?

It hardly ever crosses my mind that I'm a doctor's wife. Partly this is because Ann Arbor is a town where people aren't much defined as someone's wife or husband, but only as themselves in terms of what they can do. Partly it is because of Bob. He has never once in our life together suggested that I should behave like "a doctor's wife." I don't think either of us is really sure what that would be, and we've not found out. I am forever grateful to him for providing me with circumstances and the freedom to be what I am.

Do you see yourself as a feminist?

That's complicated. I don't see myself as a militant feminist. I'm not out to step on men's heads. But I resent the various ways that women automatically defer to men. I resent the persisting inequalities. I sometimes wonder how much feminism has truly changed our perceptions of ourselves and of men. Certainly the opportunities that have opened for women in the last fifteen years are heartening. And to see our daughters expecting to be able to do everything—well, in a way that's heartening, too. But I'm not sure they're going to be able to. I cheer for them, but I worry.

Society still influences role expectations of men and women. Do you see some of that with your husband?

Yes. He was an intern when Lisa was born. Thus, he was rarely home, and when he was, he was tired. He had very little time or energy to spend on the children in their early years, and he expected me to do it all. In a sense, that was a replication of my own childhood, but for different reasons. We deferred totally to my father. What he said, did, his schedule, and so forth absolutely determined what happened in the house, no matter what else was going on. But it wasn't merely a matter of time constraints or fatigue. It was the way the world was.

That certainly has found some attention in your books.

Yes.

We'll talk more about your writing later. Right now we want to pry a little more into your personal life. What is your house like? the neighborhood? Have you lived there long?

When we moved to Ann Arbor, I felt that I'd come home, which was odd since I had never lived any place remotely like Ann Arbor. I think what I meant was that I had arrived in a place often imagined—a college town where people thought and talked about serious things, where it was perfectly possible to go almost anywhere in dungarees, where it was fine to be anybody you felt like being. When Bob finished his residency here and began looking around the country for places to practice, I dug in my heels. By then I couldn't imagine living in a place that didn't provide that kind of freedom, so we stayed.

I began looking for a house. I found it almost at once—a slightly dilapidated white frame colonial at the edge of campus, a quintessentially Ann Arbor house. For five years, I drove past it, wondering whether it would ever be for sale. Then one day I drove past and saw piles of things on the curb, waiting for the trash people. These were the sorts of piles, I thought, that meant someone was moving, and so I stopped and knocked at the door and said, please, let us buy it.

The house was a wreck. For about three years, I painted woodwork, steamed off wallpaper, cut back bushes. But this was a love affair, and I was young. Besides, there was plenty of room for us. There was a lilac hedge out front, a family of raccoons in the storm sewer, two fireplaces, and a room entirely isolated from the rest of the house which looked like a place a person might use to write in. Evidently it also looked like an ideal bedroom for a boy, and that was what it became for many years.

We furnished the house with our parents' cast-offs because, once we'd signed a mortgage, that was all we could afford. Old rugs. Old chests. Old chairs. There was a time when I thought that one day all this would be replaced, but it never has been. How can you replace a chest of drawers that a seven-year-old scarred accidentally with his hockey stick? Once I might have but not now that the seven-year-old is grown up and gone, and the scars remind me of what it was like to have a small hockey player in the house.

So 25 years later, we are still here, in a house full of old rugs and chairs and an attic full of I-don't-know-what. About a year ago, Bob and I decided that we would probably never move, that we would never find the will and determination to clean out the attic, but we did have a yearning for something clean and stark and modern, and so we decided to build a summer cottage on a piece of property we own far north in the state—as you'd say in Michigan, at the tip of the little finger. We thought we could design it.

Designing a house is a lot like writing a book, I discovered. At first it seemed pretty simple. We'd lived in houses, after all. But our first design omitted halls; we'd forgotten we needed what amounted to logical connections. By the time we got to our second and third and fourth designs (our revisions, in other words), we were beginning to wonder if we'd bitten off more than we could chew. But the fifth plan looked pretty good to us, and we thought it would work. We hired a contractor. He began suggesting changes.

It was at this point that I had a moment of déjà vu. There was something in this man's tact, in the delicate way he made suggestions, that recalled Deborah Brodie. "We're working with an editor," I told Bob. "We'd better listen to him."

Besides designing houses, how do you spend your free time?

My inclination is to say, "What free time?" But, of course, that's silly. I have free time—just not as much as I'd expected to have at this stage in my life. I had thought that when the children were grown, there would suddenly be long afternoons for lying in a hammock. Not so. Other things turn up to fill the gap, and so far I haven't had time to buy a hammock.

But free time? I jog and walk and play tennis. I read a lot. I hardly ever watch television.

Do you volunteer in the community?

Most of my volunteering has been related to schools in one way or another: the usual PTA positions when the children were in grade school; a trustee on the board of the country day school they attended from seventh grade on; a lot of talking and reading in schools, which I do on a volunteer basis in our own community. Also, I've been part of a community enrichment program in the schools here that involves one-on-one instruction of students who are especially interested or gifted in creative writing.

Besides this, I have worked in the breakfast program for the homeless at our church and, when Ann Arbor received HUD [U.S. Department of Housing and Urban Development] funds for public housing, I was on the committee that decided how to apportion that money. At the moment I am interested in a program to help the mentally impaired (and often homeless) in the community learn marketable skills.

Other activities: cooking? gardening? sightseeing? museums? movies? theater? concerts?

Cooking? No. I am a terrible cook, and I don't care. I learned to my chagrin years ago that my children were spending their allowances to buy other mothers' cookies from their friends. When confronted with this fact, Lisa, age seven, said, "Well, I guess some people's mothers have to write books."

Gardening? Yes. I love it. I could happily spend all day in the garden pulling weeds, and often do, since we have a lot of weeds. What I especially love is wildflowers and have tried to turn our back yard into a sort of wildflower garden. But growing wildflowers is like raising children (or writing, for that matter). You've got to respect their refusal to behave the way you dream they will. Dutchman's breeches is a case in point. I have wrestled with that plant for years, trying to find a place it might deign to grow, only to discover a thriving clump in the very place I'd never have imagined would suit it. Maybe it moved by itself. Maybe a bird or squirrel moved it. Who knows? Truly, it is a lot like writing.

Also indoor gardening. I have a whole room full of pot plants in winter—mainly azaleas and orchids, cymbidiums, those wonderful stalks of butterfly flowers—but everyone has areas of insanity, and so I'm nursing a bougainvellia along.

Sightseeing? I am married to a man who is not satisfied to see the usual, the easy, or the comfortable sights that anyone can see, as he puts it. And, therefore, I have spent my traveling life searching out the cloaca maxima in Rome (which is the original ditch that drained Roman marshes in some year B.C.); the temple to Apollo at Bassae (arrived at by risking our lives); the very top of some mountain in the Lake District [in England], which we hiked to through a fog so thick that it would have been quite easy to step off into eternity at any moment; cairns in Ireland that involved pushing the car the last few hundred yards through a peat bog. In Tunisia, searching out Roman ruins, we were fired upon. I think I used to like to do the conventional thing, but I've gotten accustomed to this other, and now I don't think a sight is worth seeing if you can get to it easily, or safely, or in any comfort.

One of the traveling things we've done is to take groups of college students to Europe on three occasions—to Greece once and once each to Ireland and England—with a friend who is a professor in the English department here. On each of these trips, we traveled for a month or more, studying literature. In Greece we read Aeschylus, Sophocles, etc. In England we read Hardy. In Ireland, Yeats and Joyce. One can perfectly well read these things in Cleveland, but it is magic to read *The Mayor of Casterbridge* in Dorchester, *Tess of the d'Urbervilles* at Stonehenge, or Yeats's poetry in the shadow of his tower. And it is magic to live so many weeks with young people, to sit on an all-night ferry from Patras to Brindisi listening to their guitars (which naturally they brought instead of raincoats). I think that when I am an old woman looking back, I will remember that all-night boat ride when I have forgotten much else. I'll remember the phosphorescence on the water and the sweet-sad sound of those guitars.

Museums, movies, theaters? If you live in the Midwest, you find that every so often you get a feeling that you're living on a dry planet. When this happens to us, Bob and I go to New York and stuff ourselves with museums and plays. We don't go to musicals because they're too expensive and Bob hates them. Myself, I could happily sit through a whole weekend of them, but old marriages are built on accommodation. And so we go see things by Sam Shepherd, [Athol] Fugard, etc. And I love these too. The thing is, I love the theater. I love to be wrung out and exhilarated by make believe. When I am a long time away from New York, I read all the reviews, and often what I have read sends me to my paper and pencil with ideas for a sometime book.

Museums and galleries are mainly my thing. I hate those huge shows that museums seem to feel compelled to stage now, the ones that require dodging heads and bodies in order to see the pictures. How can you look at a Van Gogh or a Monet seriously while someone next to you is discussing her husband's gall bladder? Well, you can, but it's like concentrating in the midst of a hatch of mosquitoes. So often I prefer galleries or a museum like the Frick where I can look at a few pictures in peace.

The summer I was at Simmons I loved going to Mrs. Gardner's [the Isabella Stewart Gardner Museum] every so often to look at Piero della Francesca's *Hercules*—no heads in the way there, no gall bladders. What I want to do with a picture is to look at it long enough to share the artist's eye, to understand it. Why does this Hercules seem as flat as Cézanne's bathers, for instance? Was Piero trying to call attention to the distinction between art and reality as Cézanne seems to have been? These sorts of speculations interest me. I have an artist friend with whom I discuss such things.

Are you a social person? What are your friends like?

Several of my friends are painters, and I spend a lot of time listening to what they have to say about what they do. The first paragraph of *In Summer Light* came about through one of these conversations. I knew that I wanted an image that was both visual and sensual right at the beginning of the book, something to set the tone. I was talking with one of my friends about this, saying something of the sort, and she said, "Oh, peaches. That's the kind of thing you're getting at, isn't it?" Well, it was. Exactly. "There were peaches in a blue and white Chinese bowl . . ." An image out of Matisse and just what I wanted. Though the words are mine, the color and fragrance and texture of peaches came from her.

I am not an especially social person. I don't have anything

against being social; it's just that social life gets in the way of working. Which is probably why I choose my friends among people who are doing the same sort of thing, who understand. It is possible to say to another writer or painter, "Sorry, I can't talk right now, I'm working," and no one's feelings get hurt.

One of my best friends is Joan Blos. She and I read each other's work at all stages, and I think we help each other. At least she helps me. Joan was the one who told me eleven or twelve years ago that the book I was writing, a very early version of *The Language of Goldfish,* was not destined to be a humorous book, as I, in my utter blindness, seemed to think it was going to be. She said, "You have to take this book seriously." I can remember that I was sitting on a stool in her kitchen, and I started shaking when she said that. It was a sunny, cold fall morning, and I thought she hadn't the furnace on yet. But she had. I was shaking because I was scared to take the book seriously. I knew she was right, and I knew that meant digging further than I had ever dug before. So I sat there with chattering teeth, but she wouldn't take it back. She just said, "This could be a good book."

I guess I could say that most of the friends I value are honest in this way: they say what they mean. I have trouble with other kinds of people.

If you found yourself with a free evening, what would you do with it? What would be the perfect evening?

This is going to sound awfully dull, but it's true. My idea of the perfect evening is working in the garden until dark, if it's summer. Or building a fire and reading before it, preferably a novel, if it's winter. Going to bed about ten o'clock in any season.

But something more glamorous?

An evening I would repeat, in July in the Trastevere in Rome at a restaurant next to an ancient church whose bells tolled the hours. We were there with the children, Lisa being about 16, and an old friend happened by and joined us. He was charming to Lisa. He bought her a rose from one of the flower vendors who kept passing by. Then he bought us all some kind of brandy. We sat and sipped and listened to the bells. I watched Lisa smelling her rose and thought how like a rose she was herself, her petals unfolding.

Or an evening in New York when Bob and I took a horse cab through Central Park in a blizzard just for the fun of it.

Or go way back: I am 16. It's a Christmas dance. I have a new white silk dress and, under it, a crinoline petticoat and a corsage of red roses tied to my wrist. On my other wrist is a dance program. One of the signatures on the program is mysterious—only an initial—and I am wondering to whom it can belong. Who has signed up so mysteriously for the ninth dance with me? I was on pins and needles waiting, sure that the initial belonged to someone terrific. Then the ninth dance came around, and here came my father. I was utterly embarrassed. I thought that he must have worried I wouldn't have partners. He asked me to dance very formally. I said, "Oh, God, Daddy!" But then we waltzed. He had asked the orchestra to play one. We were the only couple on the floor who knew how to waltz, and we whirled around the floor, sliding on the dance wax, until the room was a blur and my dress was billowing.

Any of these I would gladly repeat, but, of course, they are not repeatable.

What kind of celebrations do you enjoy? On what occasions do you break out the champagne?

Most of all, I enjoy holidays that bring the family together, and that usually means Christmas. I love the weeks of preparation that go into the holiday: the cooking, the baking, the decking of the house. Sometimes I think we will sink under the weight of all the tradition, just as our Christmas tree seems sometimes on the point of collapse under the weight of ornaments collected over generations. But not a single tradition is expendable. I forget to hang mistletoe at my peril. For Christmas dinner, there can be no substitutions. There must be roast beef, a plum pudding set afire and trimmed with holly, a bûche de Noël. The same ratty old stockings are hung every year. Last thing Christmas Eve we must gather to read the story of the Nativity. Sometimes I am tired by the time the last person has gone to bed on Christmas Eve, but I like to stand in the dark after the house is finally quiet and breathe in the deep, mysterious fragrance of pine boughs and feel Christmas coming toward me just as it did when I was four and five and six, falling asleep in the pine-scented darkness in another house in another place.

Champagne? Lately we've broken it out to toast love. An engagement. A marriage last September. A thirty-fifth wedding anniversary. And the birthday of a grandmother who, miraculously, turned 85.

How would you describe yourself?

I don't know how I can describe myself. I keep coming up with contradictions. For instance, I like—need, really—a good deal of solitude, but I would be lonely without friends and family. I am happiest wearing an old pair of blue jeans, but I like pretty clothes. I love being up early in the morning, but I like to sleep late. I think that I am a reticent person until I hear myself talking. I always believe I'd like to live in the country, but the traffic passing by our house keeps me interested. How to reconcile that and come up with a description? I guess I could say that I don't want to miss out on *anything*. Maybe you can't have it all, but you can try.

What gift would you most like to receive?

More time in a day and the energy to use it.

Let's talk about your writing. In thinking about your mother and telling stories and quoting passages, we're reminded of how frequently references to other books appear in your fiction. For example, in the first chapter of The Language of Goldfish, *you describe Carrie, her trip in the elevator, and her attraction to falling. That reminded us of* Alice in Wonderland *falling down the rabbit hole.*

Oh, for heaven's sakes!

And we remembered that Alice *was a favorite book of yours.*

I read it when I was young. I've liked it much more as an adult.

Later in the novel you include part of Keats's poem "The Eve of Saint Agnes," which is a direct literary allusion. Of course, Kate works on a paper about Prospero from The Tempest *in* In Summer Light. *And you include Joseph Conrad and Emily Dickinson in* A Formal Feeling.

I'm obviously aware of the direct uses, but something like this falling—I've never thought of that.

On the jacket cover of War Work, *it says that you think children are different now. Can you talk about that a little?*

At the time I wrote that book, my own children were small. I had grown up during the Second World War, and they were growing up during Vietnam. I sometimes told them about *my* war years, about all the activities we engaged in to help "the war effort." I tried to describe the general atmosphere of those war years in this country. It all seemed very strange to them. They found it odd that anyone would support a war because there was so much negative feeling about Vietnam. And, of course, they were living in Ann Arbor, Michigan, where student and faculty protests about the war went on all the time. They were antiwar, and they couldn't understand, couldn't believe, the different outlook in my childhood.

Your three young adult novels focus on girls, and certainly they are read by girls. Do you ever envision writing something boy oriented?

I think I would have a hard time writing from a boy's point of view. For me, that would be a little bit like writing from the perspective of a Martian. The tiny nuances of feeling that interest me in my female characters would simply not be available to me were I to write about boys.

Are you interested in issues that are relevant to adolescents, or are you more focused on issues relevant to young women?

To young women, I think. I was about to say that family relationships—the sorts of relationships I like to write about—are not necessarily gender distinct. But that's nonsense. The way a boy relates to his father or his mother is substantially different from the way a girl does. That's what I mean about not being able to write from a boy's perspective. I wouldn't understand the nuances in those relationships with the same intimacy.

Do you have a sense that a happy family is a mythic notion, or are happy families possible?

Happy families are possible. Perfect families are a mythic notion. There are happier and unhappier people and, therefore, happier and unhappier families.

And what about childhood? Do you see it as an ideal state?

I don't see childhood as an ideal state, no. It may be for some people. Some people remember their childhoods with great affection. But it seems to me that childhood, in many ways, is bound to be a rocky time. I remember the misunderstandings and confusions, as well as the pleasures. I remember that there was often real pain.

Carrie, in The Language of Goldfish, *has romanticized in some way her own young childhood.*

Yes, she's idealizing it, but often when you idealize something, as Anne in *A Formal Feeling* idealizes her dead mother, it is simply refusing to look at the total picture, at other things that might be difficult. I don't think Carrie's childhood was all that ideal, but compared to what she is anticipating, it seems ideal.

*Let's talk about your work as a writer. Do you schedule a time to
write, or are you more flexible? Has the time available to you
changed dramatically over the years? Where do you work?*

When I first started, I wrote when the children were taking naps.
Then when they went to school, I'd write while they were in
school. Everything would come to a screeching halt at lunchtime
and at three o'clock. Now I always try to write in the morning,
but it takes me a while to get started. First, I either jog or walk
(I have a walking friend and a jogging friend, so this is both exercise and social life for me). When I get home, I spend a good
deal of time thinking of all the things I might do to avoid writing.
Sometimes this can go on a while. There is a particularly rich
range of distraction in summer when I add the garden chores to
the house ones, but eventually I get my cup of coffee upstairs to
Lisa's old room, which overlooks the street—and therefore provides additional distraction—and start to work for the day. I read
over what I've written the day before and spend some time revising that. This serves as a kind of pump-priming. It gets me going.
Then if it's a good day, I'll work for about four hours with total
concentration, not remembering what time it is or where I am
until I get hungry. Then I stop, have a peanut butter sandwich,
pull a few weeds, and go back for another couple of hours. If it is
a bad day, I wander around the house trying to figure out what is
giving me so much trouble, getting more and more unhappy with
myself for being so stupid. These days alternate in unpredictable
ways.

When I'm in the middle of a book, weeks pass in this way, and
the routine of the days is almost identical. When I'm teaching, I
don't try to write at all. Writing and teaching may seem to be
complementary activities, but they aren't, at least for me. They
require very different kinds of concentration, and I don't shift
back and forth easily.

The happiest writing I ever did—and I sometimes think now
that these were the happiest days I ever had—occurred during
the writing of *The Language of Goldfish*. I had been lent a friend's
house to write in. It was a wonderful small cottage with a lovely,

tiny garden. She was away for the summer. My job was to water her plants. In exchange for this small job, I had an entirely private place to work. Every morning for a whole summer, I rode my bike there, down a bumpy alley where lilac bushes were in bloom, then honeysuckle, then wild summer flowers—sweet rocket, black-eyed susans, chicory, finally asters—and I wrote one chapter a day in a delicious state of concentration and excitement. This was where I learned to prime the pump, to go over the previous day's work as a prelude to launching into the unknown.

I remember that summer with such affection. It seemed to me that the house and all the blooming things were necessary to the book. When my friend came home at the end of August, I wasn't sure I could finish the book without all that. But it was almost finished, and I did.

Oddly, now that I think about it, three of my books were written in other people's houses—ones that I housesat for a semester or two in exchange for the privilege of writing there. I am about to do the same thing this summer, and I hope that whatever mysterious effect this has had in the past will recur.

The Language of Goldfish was written longhand, as was *A Formal Feeling.* There was something almost superstitious about the feel of my hand on the paper, the look of ink or pencil on the ruled lines of a notebook. Lately I've been using a typewriter. Never a word processor—that would be like eating all my meals at McDonald's. A typewriter is technology enough for me, enough between me and what I'm writing, but it is faster. I started using a typewriter midway through the first revision of *In Summer Light,* and I think I could still show you where technology took over from hand and paper in that book. Not long ago, I said this to someone who writes and who understood immediately. I commented on the more mechanical sound of the sentences when I switched to a typewriter, and he said, "Well, it's because you don't feel the words through your body as well that way." This is true. Writing moves out through one's body onto the page. When I'm having a hard time saying something the way I want to say it, I switch back to longhand. I am beginning to think that in writing, as in painting, the involvement of the body is terribly important, even if it is only the brushing of fingers on paper.

Do you make many changes?

A tremendous number. I sent five different full manuscripts of *In Summer Light* to my editor. Five revisions.

Do you write the story from beginning to end and then go back and rework the whole thing?

Yes. I need to tell the whole story first really to see where I'm going with it. Ideas come along in the course of the writing that I'm not expecting or planning for. These will make a great difference in the direction the story ultimately goes. When I've finished a first draft, I go back over it and begin to explore what I've said— all the dead ends and blind alleys, as well as the unexpected ideas I may use. Only after that do I have some real sense of where I'm headed.

Is your pace as a writer satisfying or frustrating?

The little I can achieve in a day is very frustrating. There are days when I get a page written—a single page—then look at it the next day and say, "That's not a very good page," and one day's work goes into the wastebasket. I work very, very slowly, and that frustrates me.

Has your relationship with your editor been a good one? Have you had the same editor for all your books?

Through all the young adult novels, yes, and it's a very good relationship. We understand each other, or perhaps I should say that she understands what I'm trying to do. She has made some big additions to some of these books. For instance, in *In Summer Light,* I had written a completely different ending to the book in which Kate and her father reconcile. Deborah Brodie, my editor at Viking, said, "This ending just won't work. You've written these characters, you've created these characters, and the characters you've created would never have a reconciliation. They simply can never get on the same track." She was right. So I had to go back and rewrite the ending. In that book, the line where Kate asks Ian to take her to Boston was Deborah's. I had Kate say "I love you," or something of that sort, and Deborah said it would be much more effective to say something else. That changed the next several chapters for me because I could see she was right. We work that closely. She has that much input.

Why do you think you had Kate and her father come together at the end of that first time? Do you have a need to write (or read) a happy ending?

I felt the need to have a happy ending, yes, and not necessarily just in the book. But, as I say, it wasn't in the stars for those two people, given who they were.

What defines a young adult book?

Ah, that's tricky. Let's say a young adult novel is nearly always about an adolescent. Fine and true, but there are numberless adult novels about adolescents too. Or let's say a young adult novel deals with issues peculiar to adolescents. I can say the same thing about these adult novels. I think the difference lies in the way the story is told. An adult novel about adolescence is frequently seen from a distance; the perspective is one of an adult remembering, sifting an adolescent experience through years of maturity. The young adult novelist, on the other hand, shares the perspective of the adolescent in the book. The experiences are not remembered or sifted over time; they are lived through with the character and understood from that character's point of view and at his or her level of maturity.

With The Language of Goldfish had you decided to write a book
for an audience older than that of your picture books, or was it
simply the next story that had to be told?

I think it was the next story that had to be told. Carrie simply
appeared to me, and she interested me and without really thinking too far I started writing. I thought I was writing a humorous
book, if you can believe it. Then about midway through, or as I
was approaching the middle, I realized that what was happening
was not funny. To be afraid of growing up is a serious issue. Besides, I began to see where all this was leading. I saw that Carrie
was sufficiently upset to try something like suicide. At that point
I just stopped. I worried. This wasn't an adult novel, I thought,
but it certainly wasn't a children's book. I was entirely ignorant
of the whole field of young adult literature at the time, and I
couldn't see where this book would fit. And that's when I learned
about young adult books and that there was a place for what I'd
written.

It wasn't a conscious decision to write for a different audience
then?

No, it wasn't. The character interested me, and I followed her.
   It has always been characters who have demanded my attention. If there are two things I need in order to write a book, they
are these: a strong sense about a character and a real feeling for
the atmosphere of the story. What do the surroundings look like?
What are the predominant colors? Color is important to me—for
example, the color blue in *A Formal Feeling*. In a sense, the color
creates the atmosphere for me; it is absolutely integral to my perception of the whole book. A book has to be visual to me. I need
to be able to see the characters and setting clearly.

Are you interested in the language itself rather than the
narrative shape of the book?

Well, I'm interested in both, of course, and they are interrelated.
The story I have to tell will dictate both its own shape and lan-

guage. In the case of *The Language of Goldfish,* for instance, I wanted it clear at the beginning of the book that Carrie had pulled through, was on her way to recovery. Therefore, I needed to begin the book near the end of the story and tell the body of the story in what is really an extended flashback. This seemed the right shape for that book. Others I've written in a more strictly chronological way, though there, too, I've used flashbacks to incorporate the background information needed to round out the characters and their relationships.

In Summer Light is a book about painters, and it seemed natural to me that the language of this book should derive in large part from painting. The images are visual ones, relying on language that expresses color or light or line. I think I was more aware of the language I used in this book than in the others.

Your three young adult novels are all written in the third person. Have you ever thought about or tried to start in the first person?

Yes. I have spent the last year and a half trying to write in the first person, and I simply can't do it. It's too loose a form for me. I miss the control of a third-person narrator guiding the action, commenting obliquely, all that. I'm not saying that all this can't be done by a first-person narrator, just that I've had a devilishly hard time doing it. My first-person narrator bolted out of the barn and just started talking, and I never could get her to slow down enough to let me catch up.

Is that the hardest part about writing. Finding the framework?

For me, the hardest part is to modulate the emotion in the book, modulate the feelings. How is this character going to react to this situation? How is she going to feel? And once I know what her reaction is going to be, how is she going to express that reaction? To modulate these changes in feeling so that they flow almost like music chapter to chapter, flow and move and change believably, that's the hard part.

Does character depart when you finish writing the book?

Yes, I'd say so. I have a lingering fondness for my characters, but I don't think of them as having an ongoing existence. They end when the book ends.

A child once asked me about that. She was cross because she wanted to know what happened next—what happened to the character after the end of the book. When I told her there wasn't any next, that the character and the story ended at the same time, she got really angry. She said, "Well, I think Carrie went to high school and she met this really cool guy and later she was a famous artist in New York." I'm glad Carrie was that real to her, but, for me, Carrie will never be any older than 13.

The characters who don't leave my mind, the ones I still wonder about, are those that have been less developed in the books. Kate's parents, for instance. I could be interested in writing a book about them. I'd like to know more about what makes Kate's mother tick. I've never been absolutely certain, but I think I could find out. That's where an adult novel might come in sometime. I might try writing about Kate's parents.

Earlier you mentioned that you're working on a book about sister relationships. How is that work going?

Well, it's going. Actually, there are two books at present: a young adult novel and a biography of Willa Cather, which Bantam has asked me to write as part of a series of biographies of women that Barnard College is sponsoring. The biography is still in the research stage, and I won't start writing until I've finished the novel. And when will that be? I'd hope by the end of the winter.

Are you satisfied with the body of work you've created?

No, if you mean am I satisfied to sit back and rest with what I've done. No, not at all. Am I satisfied with the individual books? Yes and no. Once in a while, I'll go back and look at one of them and I'll say, "That's not bad." Other times I'll say, "You know, really you've learned something since you wrote that one." Satisfied? Yes and no. I hope I can do more. I hope I can do it better.

Do you have a favorite?

Yes. *The Language of Goldfish.* I feel closest to that one. I had to learn a lot about writing to write that book. It was quite different from anything I'd written before, and I had to struggle for it, struggle for every sentence. I suppose that's why it has a special place in my heart.

What have you always wanted to write but have not written?

I think I've written whatever I've wanted to eventually. Sometimes it has taken a while to learn how to write it. The *how* is more a problem than the *what.*

Do you visit schools to talk with your reading audience?

Yes, and I always request that the group has read the books, or at least one of them. If they don't know the books, why will they be interested in listening to me? When they have read the books, there are really good questions, and we can have truly useful conversations about writing. I think I gain as much from these conversations as they do. It's a way to keep in touch with the people I'm writing for and about.

Often these conversations begin with a question about how much in the book is true, how much really happened, and with my insisting that fiction is fiction no matter how close it sometimes comes to touching fact. What we write comes out of our own experience, of course. Where else would it come from? But the job of the writer of fiction is to take that raw material from experience and shape it into something that has meaning and significance beyond the simple event, beyond the germ of fact that inspired it.

We talk about the difference between life and fiction. We talk about the way that a fictional character exists only within the fiction and has no life outside it. And we talk about the ways in which fictional characters *are* real. I try to explain that once I've created a character—given her her personality—I'm stuck with that. There are certain things she will never do or say, certain ways she will invariably behave. In that, she becomes as real to me as a friend. I know her strengths and limitations. I know what I can and cannot do with her. The reality of her character becomes a limitation on my freedom, even though, in truth, she is purely imagined, and by me.

Is it The Language of Goldfish *that is read most?*

I'd say that and *In Summer Light* are most read. I happen to think that *A Formal Feeling* is technically the best of my books, but I don't think it's ever been as popular as the other two. Perhaps it's a little chilly, a little standoffish. The purely technical things that I like about it may not be the sorts of things that would make it popular.

Aside from school visits, do you ever hear from your readers? Do they write to you?

I hear from readers fairly regularly, and I always try to answer these letters, remembering how I used to write to authors I liked as a child, hoping against hope they'd write to me in return.

The letters I receive seem to fall into two categories: those wanting information about me and my books for school projects; those that come from readers who simply seem to want to make contact. The latter are, of course, the ones that go to my heart because I can so clearly remember wanting to make that kind of contact with someone who was doing what I hoped, one day, to do. "I love to write," these letters say. Or, "I am trying to write a novel." Or simply, "I liked your book. I wish you'd write to me." And so I do.

"Where do your ideas come from?" This is the question most frequently asked and the hardest to answer. No matter what I answer, I am telling only part of the truth—not purposely but because I really don't know the full answer. Ideas come out of the life I've led and the thoughts I've thought and the feelings I've had—but what kind of answer is that? Vague, general, not very helpful—but as close as I'm likely to get to an answer that is true.

What I wish they'd ask are questions having to do with the craft of writing. I'd like to have an occasion to explain that writing is about 99 percent hard work—revising and rethinking and trying to get as close as you can to what it is you want to say, and failing. I think there is some general belief that writers sit down and whip off a chapter because they're inspired. Well, maybe some do. Not me. I'm more like a carpenter, sawing and planing and sanding a piece of raw wood, and being many times disappointed in the result before I get a little bit right.

I would love some day to be asked to give a talk on the subject of revising because I think that's what writing is mainly about. But nobody asks for this subject. It is the descent of the Muse that seems to be of interest, and that's the least important part. We are all of us visited by the Muse off and on. It's getting out the sandpaper that makes a book finally.

More time in schools ought to be devoted to learning the craft, the tools that writing requires. All this stress on "creativity" seems silly to me. If you can't think logically or spell or write a coherent sentence, you are in the same position as the artist who has never learned to draw or the composer who is unfamiliar with scales.

Are the technical aspects and the crafted elements of the novel teachable? Can one really "teach" creative writing?

I think so. I think you can teach a student something, particularly when you are working on revisions. Obviously you can't teach someone to be "creative," but you can look at a finished first draft and begin to show a student something about shaping, something about the craft of writing. You can do, at this point, very much the kind of thing an editor does. We all learn from editors.

So, in some ways, you can teach creative writing by teaching careful reading?

Oh, yes. I think a wide background in reading is essential to writing. To have read a tremendous amount, to have the language in your bones and blood, that's how you learn to write. That way you begin to know how sentences should sound, how other writers have created and solved problems. Reading is the real apprenticeship. That's how you learn.

2. Charting a Course

Zibby Oneal is best known for her three young adult novels: *The Language of Goldfish, A Formal Feeling,* and *In Summer Light.* She has also published two picture books, two novels for young readers, and, for a young audience, a biography of Grandma Moses and a short historical novel. Although these latter works are less successful than the young adult books, they focus on themes and issues she explores more fully later. Connections to the author's life that are apparent in these books become more deeply and firmly embedded in the three young adult novels.

As Oneal's two children grew, the ages of her characters also increased. Her first characters, Zoe and Rosie from *War Work,* are 10 and 8 years old, respectively, just slightly younger than her own children, to whom the book is dedicated. *The Improbable Adventures of Marvelous O'Hara Soapstone* features Lemon and Iris, two sisters close to the same age. As her children moved into young adulthood, Oneal's characters also grew into adolescence: Carrie is 13 in *The Language of Goldfish,* Anne is 16 in *A Formal Feeling,* and Kate is 17 in *In Summer Light.* Oneal acknowledges this succession: "My characters aged along with [my children]. Eventually, everyone reached adolescence, but my characters remained there, because I found I was deeply interested in exploring this brief time of life, these few years when everything is in the process of becoming."[1]

These characters are recognizable in some form from Oneal's life. Like the young Oneal, Zoe experiences frustration and impatience with her younger sister. Simultaneously, waves of love and protectiveness sweep over her. Zoe wants to be a writer; she has "been thinking about writing a novel since she was seven."[2] Possessing an active imagination and a writer's flair for the dramatic, she conjures possible headlines that could accompany her actions. Upon discovering packed crates hidden in a neighbor's basement, Zoe imagines the lead: "MYSTERIOUS EXPLOSION DESTROYS FAMILY   Nothing left" (*WW,* 197). Maude, one of the title characters in the picture book *Maude and Walter,* fantasizes about a 100-foot-tall, larger-than-life hero who acts as the companion and friend her brother is not.

The picture books and novels for young children rely heavily on plot. Unlike the reflective Carrie, Anne, and Kate, these younger characters are always doing things. Age-appropriate physical activity characterizes their play. Zoe and Rosie tag along with Joe on his trips to deliver tin cans to the Armory. They organize exclusive but short-lived clubs. Their lust for adventure drives them. Like Harriet the spy, they eavesdrop and snoop on neighbors, frequently misunderstanding what they hear.

Like Fern in *Charlotte's Web,* Lemon and Iris are soon upstaged by the pig they care for. Like Wilbur, Marvelous O'Hara Soapstone has the potential to be a prize pig. The story follows Marvelous O'Hara and the Soapstones as they seek solutions to outrageous problems on their quest for a blue ribbon.

Turtle and Snail, Oneal's only writing with no human child characters, presents five illustrated vignettes about the evolving friendship between the title characters. Much like Arnold Lobel's Frog and Toad, Turtle and Snail charm new readers as they engage in and reminisce about their good times together.

Maude is tested by her brother's rejection of her friendship. In *Maude and Walter,* she invents a variety of cunning ways to win her brother's companionship, and ultimately she wins his friendship too.

Friendship becomes one of the primary themes linking the two picture books and early novels with Oneal's young adult novels. Snail openly declares his need for a friend: "'I want a friend,' Snail said. 'I am lonely.'"[3] In a learning-to-read format, Snail's meeting with Turtle and the friendship they create fulfill this desire for a friend. Young children who work to establish similar bonds with their peers recognize both Snail's yearning and his joy. Maude expends physical and creative energies in her mission to gain her brother's company. Her relentlessness is rewarded when Walter begins to see his sister as both companion and friend. Lemon and Iris do not suffer from the sibling rejection Maude experiences with Walter. Rather, they are usually pictured together—playing games, christening pigs, setting up lemonade stands, or just enjoying each other. The limited two-person neighborhoods of Turtle and Snail, Maude and Walter, Lemon and Iris expand somewhat in *War Work*. Zoe has a thorny and uneasy friendship with her sister, Rosie. However, Joe Bunch, the boy from "down at the end of the block" (*WW*, 13), is truly Zoe's friend. She admires Joe and wants to impress him. Mutual respect characterizes their relationship. In trying to dismantle a spy ring, Zoe and Joe work together, equally inventing the game and investing in playing it well.

For Carrie, Anne, and Kate, friendship loses the frivolity of play. For these three troubled and burdened young adults, friends become anchors, "rudder[s] steadying [their] confusion" (*ISL*, 143). Carrie remembers acutely the friendship she left behind in Chicago when her family moved. Mrs. Ramsay, Carrie's art teacher, always supported Carrie; now, during Carrie's recuperation, Mrs. Ramsay provides new strength and understanding. By the novel's close, Carrie's growing self-confidence enables her to reach out to Daniel Spangler and make new friends. Easygoing, energetic Laura complements Anne Cameron, a remote and standoffish girl. In Laura's relaxed nature, Anne sees the simplicity missing from her own overly complex perspective. Leah, Kate's roommate, possesses many of Laura's qualities: charming, affable, direct. Kate welcomes Leah's breeziness. In their relationship, nothing is forbidden; Kate confides in Leah, and Leah listens attentively.

In all but one of Oneal's books for children and young adults, the family occupies a central role. Throughout, the nuclear family—mother, father, and two children—remains whole and intact. Given that Oneal is writing from the early seventies through the eighties and on into the nineties, this recurring pattern of whole family is somewhat of an anomaly. Unlike so many other contemporary protagonists, Oneal's children and adolescents are not latchkey kids or the by-products of failed marriages. Clearly Oneal's own past informs this vision of family in her fiction. In *Maude and Walter*, the parents may be generally off-stage, but they provide a reliable background. The Soapstones engage in hilarious schemes and outrageous antics with their children; all play together. In *War Work,* Zoe's parents provide a loving home for their children, supplying not only guidance but also support and comfort. Zoe and Rosie experience sibling rivalry, but their genuine affection for each other triumphs.

Carrie's family may not understand her and may struggle with her problems, but individually and collectively they demonstrate their love for her. Anne Cameron's family history is complicated by the possibility of divorce. Her parents' marriage has difficulties threatening its stability. Still, Oneal's pattern of an intact marriage is valid. The Camerons do not give up on their marriage easily; they make it work. After his wife's death, Mr. Cameron attempts to reassemble a nuclear family with Dory. Spencer's understanding of his sister, Anne, allows him to tolerate her unpleasantness to him, his father, and Dory. He provides brotherly comfort and support as she struggles with her mother's death and her changing family. Although Kate and her younger sister, Amanda, are separated by nearly 10 years in age, this family replicates the pattern. The father may be famous and the mother traditional, but they are constants in the lives of their children.

Grandma Moses: Painter of Rural America is Zibby Oneal's single piece of nonfiction. Despite this difference, the work shares strong thematic similarities with her fiction. Simplicity and clarity of prose combine with freshness and originality to create a highly readable biography from the "Women of Our Times" series. In language and scope just right for children ages 7 to 11, Oneal captures the human qualities of the renowned painter. *Grandma Moses* once again demonstrates Oneal's ability to give life and substance to characters. This true story is placed in a historical rather than a fictional setting rich in vivid detail. All biographers must select the relevant aspects of their subject's life. Oneal seems particularly attuned to her audience, choosing to highlight and describe those parts of Grandma Moses's life that speak to the young child. For example, Grandma Moses "squeeze[s] paint from the tube directly onto the brush like toothpaste."[4] Not only do Oneal's images enliven the text, but so do the images she extracts from Grandma Moses's own words. Oneal's obvious interest in art and color, evident in her fictional works, also plays a key role in this biography. She portrays Grandma Moses at her wedding in "a hat trimmed with a pink feather" (*GM,* 18) and at the end of her life as "a tiny old woman . . . [with] white hair in a knot on top of her head, a black ribbon at her throat" (*GM,* 56); she describes an early scene of "a bright yellow lake, as if seen in sunlight" (*GM,* 25). Indeed, even writing about Grandma Moses underscores Oneal's interest in painterly things: "If I were not a writer, I'd like to be a painter. In my novels, my characters sometimes are. I'm not sure I agree with Grandma that anyone can paint. But I'm certain that anyone can learn, by looking, to share the artist's eye" (*GM,* 58).

When asked to contribute to the "Women of Our Times" series, Oneal suggested Grandma Moses as a subject. Oneal infuses her view of the artist with a deep commitment to family, a theme echoed in her fiction. As a child, Grandma Moses, named Anna Mary, was an integral member of a large farming family. One of 10 children, she enjoyed a friendly, competitive relationship with her active siblings, especially the three brothers closest to her age. Oneal develops this child's special relationship with each of her parents. Initially a rebel, Anna Mary eventually grew to value her mother's instructions in caring for farm, home, and family.

She "remembered her father as a dreamer, and as a lover of beauty. He was himself something of a painter" (*GM,* 10). From him, she gained her interest in painting: "Like her father, Anna Mary loved beautiful things. She loved color—the blue and purple wildflowers she found in the spring, the amber color of home-made soap, the pink apron with pockets her mother made her" (*GM,* 12).

In *A Long Way to Go* (1990) Oneal recounts a historical event through a story. She places the suffrage movement in the house-hold of eight-year-old Lila, whose grandmother has been jailed for picketing on behalf of women's right to vote. The family serves as a microcosm for society at large. Lila's father is angry at his mother for her political activities, believing that women need not have the right to vote because men accept that privilege as a fam-ily responsibility. His wife conforms to his opinion and remains politically inactive. Initially intrigued by the discrepancy between her parents' position and her grandmother's, Lila develops her own sense of political involvement.

This slim volume runs only 54 pages, including 10 full-page illustrations, and is designed specifically for readers ages 7 to 11. Within these parameters, Oneal crafts an engaging, dramatic, and compelling tale that evokes strong family connections for the author: "Women had had the right to vote for only fourteen years when I was born. My grandmother had been denied the right for most of her life. When I think of the suffrage movement in this way, it seems like history that has only just finished happening."[5] Oneal invests Lila's story with the same immediacy, and she im-bues the telling with the details, descriptions, and metaphors rec-ognizable to her readers.

A brief afterword chronicles the movement's important names and dates, but it is Lila who feels and communicates to readers the fundamental ideals behind the Nineteenth Amendment. She experiences first-hand inequalities that stem solely from her gen-der. She is expected to wear white gloves, and not to perform cart-wheels, shout, nor sell newspapers. Her education is of minimal importance, while her brother's is of primary concern. Every bit an eight-year-old child, Lila senses the injustices as an eight-year-old would even while she begins to understand the issue as it extends beyond herself.

The story's dramatic confrontation and subsequent resolution grow intrinsically from the dynamics between Lila and her father. Like Anne Cameron of *A Formal Feeling,* Lila genuinely cares about her father and he about her. Curious and energetic, Lila wants to attend a protest parade with her grandmother. He forbids it. Lila's passion and knowledge during a conversation with her father both reveal her sense of injustice and enable him to see how seriously she wants to participate. Papa not only listens to but also hears Lila, even calling her words "quite a speech" (*LW,* 42). Because of her, he changes his mind.

Age-appropriate use of detail and metaphor reinforce the story's believability for young readers. Lila engages in one-upmanship when she sells newspapers on the street corner; she wants to sell more and sell faster than her male counterpart. When told she can attend the parade, "then right there, in the middle of her bedroom, stark naked, she turned a cartwheel" (*LW,* 43). Readers revel in Lila's unabashed joy. This contrasts directly with an earlier description of her as restricted: "Lila looked down at her high-button shoes, at her long, scratchy stockings that were wrinkled at the knees, at the shadow of her hair bow like a big butterfly on the sidewalk" (*LW,* 4). Children certainly identify with Lila's discomfort. The butterfly shadow subtly suggests freedom—the freedom every child wants, the freedom Lila wants from the restrictions of her society, and the freedom fought for by the suffragettes.

Other similes speak to a child's experiential frame of reference. Seeing her grandmother on a soapbox, "Lila thought she looked like a queen" (*LW,* 17). Oneal also writes in eloquent metaphor, at one point describing twilight as a time when "lights blossomed in shop windows" (*LW,* 33).

Vivid use of color enhances the visual imagery of this book. Houses are not simply houses; they are brownstones. Lila wears white gloves and chooses a red jawbreaker for herself. During the parade, a tomato splatters against Lila, leaving "red pulp and yel-

low seeds all over her stockings" (*LW,* 48). Lila, like the suffra-
gette marchers, takes yellow as emblematic of the cause.

This most recent book bridges Zibby Oneal's work for younger
readers and her young adult novels. As Oneal matures as a
writer, her fiction focuses increasingly on issues central to family
relationships. Set against the instabilities of World War II, *War
Work* portrays a safe, insulated family that for the most part is
untroubled. Similarly in *The Improbable Adventures of Marvelous
O'Hara Soapstone,* problems come from outside the family. *A
Long Way to Go* brings political issues from the outside into the
family arena. *The Language of Goldfish* presents an upwardly
mobile family that appears happy to outsiders. An integral part
of Carrie's difficulty stems from her own unhappiness and her
family's inability to accept imperfection. With her next novel, *A
Formal Feeling,* Oneal narrows her focus in the family. Anne's
story intensifies and magnifies the tensions inherent in mother-
daughter relationships. Keeping the same limited perspective,
Oneal turns to a complicated father-daughter relationship in *In
Summer Light.* The family moves from being a comfortable setting—a backdrop against which other action takes place—to the
very arena of the novel's central conflict. This telescopic perspective allows Oneal to probe deeply and to achieve fresh insights.

3. Learning the Language

In *The Language of Goldfish* (1980), Zibby Oneal's first novel for young adults, 13-year-old Carrie Stokes is on the brink of adolescence. Carrie actively resists growing up. The novel recalls the events preceding Carrie's attempted suicide and traces the initial steps of her recovery.

Carrie's journey to wellness is peopled with individuals who hinder her and those who help her. Carrie's upper-middle-class family has all the markings of stability and normality. Her mother and father have a good marriage and obviously care about their children. Her older sister and younger brother complete the family constellation. Oneal's adept character portrayals provide substance and depth to these seemingly stereotypic characters as she gives Carrie, and readers, an opportunity to examine these family members as individuals who play important roles in Carrie's illness and recovery. Beyond her immediate family, Carrie finds support in her relationships with Dr. Ross, her therapist, and Mrs. Ramsay, her art teacher, who both recognize Carrie's uniqueness and her struggle.

Carrie's dis-ease in a world where normal teenagers chew gum and go to the dentist, not the therapist, subtly pervades the novel from its opening pages. Regardless of the third-person narrator, the reader is immediately and consistently aware of Carrie's thoughts. In the opening chapter, Carrie quietly, almost anonymously, rides a train to the office of Dr. Ross, a trip she repeats daily. The physical journey mimics the larger psychological journey she must make to feel, not just act, "like a normal teenager."[1] In this first passage, Oneal develops a strong sense of the tension in Carrie's life: the struggle between normalcy and abnormalcy, the incongruity between appearances and actuality. Carrie's focus is not on her destination but on her geometry book.

Carrie contrasts the cold certainty of mathematics to the warmth and passion of poetry. Carrie's companions on the journey are the dead leaves of fall and the chilled air of oncoming snow. She seems unable to identify a middle ground where the harsh extremities of winter and summer are tempered by the relieving changes of fall and spring.

Carrie's trip to see Dr. Ross is not easy for her. This trip symbolizes her struggle toward sanity. Carrie must go from her family home, an isolated place that has been the scene of her "un-doing," to Dr. Ross's office on the twenty-third floor, the entire twenty-third floor, of an office building in the city. In contrast to her home, the doctor's office is an island of refuge, a place of healing. This daily trip requires transportation by the train, then cab, and finally the elevator. All three modes of transport are in self-contained, enclosed vehicles, cocoons of a sort, that protect and deliver Carrie safely. As she approaches her destination, the doctor's office specifically or her stability in symbolic terms, her fear of failure increases.

Oneal reveals Carrie's fears in the action of the elevator, which shakes and shivers violently as it rises. Indeed, even as she rises, Carrie considers gently falling down the elevator shaft, spiraling downward like a leaf on a pillowed current of air and landing softly. Yet despite her fears, despite her attraction to the fall, Carrie calls the elevator and embarks on the strenuous journey upward.

The opening passage states clearly the fact of Carrie's illness and her desire to get better. She keeps her appointments with the therapist despite her fears. Dr. Ross has become someone in whom she trusts and to whom she regularly turns for guidance as she works to become well. With him, she begins her journey toward health even as she "assembles her first sentence" (*LG*, 10).

These initial pages reveal Carrie's ambivalence regarding her relationship with her mother. Mrs. Stokes refuses to name Carrie's attempted suicide as an act by an unbalanced person. Rather, she "prettie[s] the truth" (*LG*, 9) and refers to Carrie merely as "unwell." This tendency to deny the truth of Carrie's instability stands in stark contrast to Carrie's need for accuracy. Not only is it in character for Carrie to identify her condition precisely, but also she can become whole and healthy again only after naming, and thereby controlling, her craziness. These first pages foreshadow the motifs, themes, characters, and some of the controversies that develop in the novel.

As Carrie begins to tell her story, the novel's structure recalls the shape of J. D. Salinger's *The Catcher in the Rye*. Readers meet the hospitalized Holden Caulfield as he pieces together his recent past.

> If you really want to hear about it, the first thing you'll probably want to know is where I was born, and what my lousy childhood was like, and how my parents were occupied and all before they had me, and all that David Copperfield kind of crap, but I don't feel like going into it, if you want to know the truth. In the first place, that stuff bores me, and in the second place, my parents would have about two hemorrhages apiece if I told anything pretty personal about them. They're quite touchy about anything like that, especially my father. They're *nice* and all, but they're also touchy as hell. Besides, I'm not going to tell you my whole goddam autobiography or anything. I'll just tell you about this madman stuff that happened to me around last Christmas just before I got pretty run-down and had to come out here and take it easy.[2]

Carrie, like Holden, is in a therapeutic setting as she begins to trace the "madman stuff" that happened to her. Unable to name it, Carrie refers to her first frightening episode as a dizzy spell. Carrie's story unfolds chronologically from this specific point at the beginning of her illness to the present time in the doctor's office. Unlike Holden, who is not interested in or capable of relating his childhood, Carrie's recollections of the recent past trigger memories of a more distant past, memories of isolated events and moments from her childhood.

In both past and present, the fall and winter prove difficult times for Carrie Stokes. Like Holden Caulfield, whose downfall begins at Christmas, holidays are stressful times for Carrie. She attempts suicide on Thanksgiving weekend, and the day before Christmas Eve she anxiously returns home from the hospital. The structure of the novel is closely tied to Carrie's remembrances of these times and to her recollections of other special occasions that have proved unsettling: the return to school, the school dance, an art exhibit.

The seasonal frame intensifies and speaks symbolically to Carrie's instability. Like the autumn leaves that float and flutter, Carrie feels suspended, groundless, helplessly falling like Alice in Wonderland down a bottomless rabbit hole with nothing to hold onto and only her own words for company. Carrie notices the tumbling leaves everywhere around her, from outside the window in her English class to "the bottom of the garden, away from the house. There were leaves floating. . . . Carrie lay down and watched them" (*LG*, 27). She pictures her older, confident sister, Moira, as "spinning away like a bright yellow leaf" (*LG*, 27). It is the action of the fall of the leaf, its abstract movement "propelled by an air current she couldn't even feel" (*LG*, 27), that she strives to convey in her drawings. She discards the leaf itself as uninteresting and yearns to give shape to the spiral of downward motion. Unconsciously, it is her own floating, her own fall, that Carrie wants to capture. In depicting it, perhaps she will gain control over it.

While Oneal portrays Carrie's obsession with the falling leaves directly in the novel's text, she allows cold, winter, and snow to operate as images within the text, images of which Carrie is not consciously aware but that beckon readers' speculation. The leaves of autumn eventually give way to falling snow. Carrie welcomes the cold breath of chilled wintry air. Winter offers her the allure of hibernation, a chance to secret herself away and to stop her fall. Snow blankets, masking the individuality of things as it covers all equally, shapelessly. This anonymity offers Carrie refuge from the change and growth inevitable in adolescence.

This theme of stasis versus change resonates throughout the novel. Carrie remembers things past and holds them unchanged. Almost like photographs, they becomes treasures to be reexamined and cherished. She prefers to remember her mother as she was when they lived in Hyde Park. Prior to their move to Northpoint, Mrs. Stokes functioned primarily as homemaker and mother. Carrie's images are of her mother cooking while she and her sister looked on from nearby stools. This sense of her happy childhood is now absent. In their new home, Carrie sees Mrs. Stokes as more socially aware. The housework and cooking are now the housekeeper's job. Mrs. Stokes wants to educate Carrie in the social graces. She wants her to take dancing lessons, wear the right clothes, have the right hair style. Because "good" families do not have mentally troubled children, Mrs. Stokes identifies Carrie's illness as anemia due to lack of nutritious breakfasts.

More affluent now, the family has a lawn instead of a sidewalk. Their house is larger than the apartment that Carrie affectionately recalls—large enough, in fact, to provide each child with a separate bedroom. Carrie and Moira no longer share a room, nor do they continue to share the childhood games of roller-skating, rope-jumping, and hopscotch. Bereft of these pastimes, Carrie clings to the last invention she and Moira co-create: the island and the language of goldfish. Not yet having met other children in Northpoint, their discovery of a fishpond with "an island of rocks in the middle" (*LG*, 15) stimulates their imaginations. The girls fantasize themselves as part of the island, able to paddle to it on a drifting leaf or ride to it on the backs of inhabitant goldfish with which they can communicate. This island remains Carrie's most cherished memory, beyond which she does not want to move. The island is Carrie's never-never land where things hold still, never changing, always staying the same. But Moira has left behind childhood games and tells Carrie that "she can't go on behaving like a little kid" (*LG*, 37), still caring about the goldfish. It "used to be fun when we were little girls, but we aren't little girls now" (*LG*, 37). Unlike Moira, Carrie cannot yet separate play from reality. She wants to hold onto and live in the fantasies of her childhood.

In addition to resisting these psychological advances away from childhood and toward adolescence, Carrie actively resents her bodily changes. Moira continues to push Carrie to acknowledge the fact of her growing up. Leaving the goldfish and the island behind is one step she insists Carrie take. She also forces Carrie to look carefully at her physical self. Moira points out to Carrie the inadequacy of her t-shirt and the necessity of a bra. Carrie has not been blind to her physical development; bathing forces her to see her naked self: "She studied herself under the water. She was changing. Most of the changing had come since Christmas. It hadn't taken very long. It made her feel strange to have these things happening. It was as if her body had decided to take a direction of its own without her consent. Irritably she pulled a washcloth off the rack and spread it over her" (*LG*, 127). This particular bath, in which Carrie planned to luxuriate, has become uncomfortable, even scary. She wants to bind her emerging breasts to prevent their growth.

As Carrie wants to deny her maturing body, she also panics when faced with adult sexuality. When Mrs. Ramsay invites Carrie on a trip with her to the Art Institute, Carrie eagerly accepts. Unfortunately, the experience goes awry, and unnamed anxiety taints Carrie's anticipated pleasure. In the art nouveau exhibit, the forceful sensuality of the work overwhelms her. Aubrey Beardsley's sinuous, tantalizing use of line entrances her. She reacts to the line in an abstract way. Once she mutely recognizes the power of sex Beardsley portrays in *Salome with the Head of John the Baptist,* she is unable to discuss the exhibit with Mrs. Ramsay, who tries to elaborate on the powerful nature of sex. Carrie first tries to block out her voice, to block out the truth of what she's saying, "to hear the snow" (*LG*, 48). Finally, she screams and runs from such adult knowledge.

Carrie perceives childhood as an unburdened stage of life. Her memories center on playing games. She shares marbles with Tanya and creates the language of goldfish with Moira. When recalling anxious moments of childhood, such as seeing her mother cry, Carrie becomes distraught. She cannot integrate the unpleasant experiences of her own childhood with her mistaken notion that childhood is consistently joyous.

While Moira strives to pull Carrie toward adolescence and adulthood, her younger brother Duncan's influence is much more subtle. As Carrie watches him, she considers him still enmeshed in the world of childhood, the world in which she wants to remain. Like Holden Caulfield's relationship with his sister, Phoebe, Carrie yearns to be as innocent as she perceives Duncan to be. Carrie wants to duplicate the carefree pleasure she assumes Duncan has when they frolic in the snow together. But like Holden, Carrie's perceptions of Duncan are false, skewed by her subconscious yearnings. In reality, Duncan's play is not totally innocent: he plays ice hockey, an aggressive game even for young children, and keeps a set of free weights. Weight lifting and muscle building suggest Duncan's interest in growing into manhood, not remaining a child. In thinking Duncan is a child, Carrie ignores evidence that he has grown beyond nursery games. Like Holden, Carrie cannot catch her sibling as he approaches the precipice of adulthood.

In her interactions with Duncan, Carrie does not realize that she often behaves like an adult. Just prior to her suicide attempt, Duncan's hockey team enters a semifinal round of championship play. The elation Duncan feels dissolves when Moira and his parents reveal they have other plans and cannot attend the game to watch him play. Perceiving Duncan's disappointment, Carrie immediately offers her support and agrees to attend the game. When building the snow fort with Duncan, Carrie begins to feel uncomfortable. She is cognizant of his pleasure in the snow, and she does not share it. Having moved somewhat beyond this part of childhood, Carrie prefers a warm bath to cold, wet mittens.

Ambivalence characterizes Carrie's relationships with her family members. She both wants and rejects Moira. With Duncan, she acts as both child and adult. She sees her parents as both protectors and abandoners. Excited about entering a drawing competition and wanting to awaken their interest in her art, Carrie shares a series of abstract drawings with them. Their comments that the drawings are "interesting" make her feel "clumsy and awkward" (*LG,* 34). Their struggle to understand the drawings deflates Carrie's confidence in her work, leaving her feeling alien and abandoned.

After a frightening dizzy spell in which "things suddenly slipped sideways, . . . inside [Carrie's] head, colors—queer colored shapes—began to tumble around" (*LG,* 12), Carrie runs to her father for help. When he greets her at his medical clinic, he "seemed suddenly enormous . . . like someone else in his long white coat" (*LG,* 49). To her, he is a knight in shining armor with the capacity to save her. When she tries to convey the enormity of the confusion she feels, he tells her that her experience is quite typical of girls her age, perhaps aggravated by some anemia. By not giving Carrie the acknowledgment that something is indeed psychologically wrong with her, Dr. Stokes abandons Carrie to her illness.

On the ride home from the clinic, Carrie reaches out to her mother, blatantly confiding in her the fear that she is going crazy. Mrs. Stokes's dismissal of Carrie's illness as improper eating or anemia is another abandonment.

Even as Carrie's parents fail her, Carrie perceives that she too fails them. In many ways, Carrie is not the daughter her mother wants. Unlike Moira, whose social facility Mrs. Stokes applauds, Carrie finds social interactions difficult. She puts off signing up for the junior dances, a decision that both baffles and annoys her mother. Carrie's interests lie with her artistic pursuits; Mrs. Stokes is more focused on the material aspects of her daughter's life. She prefers that Carrie get a flattering haircut and shop for stylish clothes rather than concentrate on art and math. When Carrie's father comments that a friend of hers has a pretty face and therefore will never need to comprehend the mathematical concepts she learns in school, he reveals the value he places on having a daughter who is attractive and popular rather than intelligent and talented.

At first look, Carrie's mother wants everything pristine and precise. Her life and her home have no place for disorder or complications—even the inconvenience of an unstable daughter. But after Carrie's suicide attempt reveals the depth of her illness, her parents provide the extensive medical and psychological attention she needs. When she returns home from the hospital during the Christmas holidays, Mrs. Stokes strives to make room for this abnormal child. Carrie's favorite Christmas ornament is a tattered angel that her mother long ago deemed inappropriate. But when Carrie takes it out and places it in the living room on the mantle among the ordered shiny, new ornaments, Mrs. Stokes notices but does not remove the shabby decoration. During the family tree trimming, Carrie's reflection on "the angel and herself . . . [both of] them a little ragged" (*LG,* 94) reveals her new-found sense of family acceptance.

Perhaps Carrie's chief supporter is Mrs. Ramsay, the art teacher with whom she has weekly private instruction. On her Saturday visits to Mrs. Ramsay's home, Carrie captures some of what she left behind when her family moved to Northpoint, some of the carefree childhood she remembers. Mrs. Ramsay, dressed in "jeans and a baggy man's cardigan" (*LG,* 105), and her messy, somewhat chaotic household, offer Carrie comfort and stability. Her madness does not penetrate this fortress of acceptance and familiarity.

Unlike Carrie's parents, Mrs. Ramsay listens to Carrie's struggle to describe the confusion in her head. She does not attribute it to anemia; rather, she trusts Carrie to know when something is wrong. She quietly attends to Carrie's words as the adolescent tries to puzzle out what's happening to her. Mrs. Ramsay's acceptance of Carrie not only confirms her sense of displacement but also empowers her to risk self-expression and self-exploration in her art.

Mrs. Ramsay clearly thinks that Carrie has artistic talent that needs to be nurtured and developed. She comments that Carrie's black-and-white studies of abstract movements show promise, but she considers them simply "marking-time pictures" (*LG,* 115). Carrie observes that these pattern drawings lack the warmth conveyed by Mrs. Ramsay's work. The lifelessness of her own drawings disturbs Carrie. She too recognizes her readiness to progress beyond visually rendering the mathematical precision of observed patterns.

The evolution of Carrie's art reflects her emotional unraveling and her steps to recovery. Her art moves from symptomatic abstract representation of downward falling motion depicted in black and white to naturalistic watercolors of an island. Her initial attempt to draw the island is not a controlled series of clean pencil strokes but a charcoal sketch, quickly and carelessly made. As she moves into watercolors, the pictures include greater detail and clarity. "It was as if the cliffs were slowly emerging from mist, as if morning sun were burning off a haze" (*LG*, 152). Eventually, she tires of painting the island and begins to draw people. For Carrie, who has wanted desperately to escape her own bodily changes, being interested in drawing "figures and faces" (*LG*, 152) marks maturation in terms of both her art and her psychological well-being.

Ambivalence plays a key role in Carrie's relationship with Mrs. Ramsay too. Carrie cannot unite the Mrs. Ramsay who finds sensuality and sex powerful attractions with the homey Mrs. Ramsay who has two rambunctious children. Having never met Mr. Ramsay, Carrie assumes it is he Mrs. Ramsay sketches and that it is he with whom she sees Mrs. Ramsay in a taxi one day. Carrie doubts, and then ignores, the rumors she hears about Mrs. Ramsay's adultery and divorce. As Carrie enlarges her sketches to make room for increasingly more detail, she must also expand her perception of Mrs. Ramsay to include behaviors that confuse and frighten her. Unlike running from the provocative Beardsley drawings, Carrie makes room for her own ambivalence in her love for Mrs. Ramsay.

As Carrie begins to recognize and accept others as they are— Moira, Duncan, her parents, Mrs. Ramsay—she begins to know and like herself more. With the knowledge that she did not place at all in an earlier art competition, Carrie prepares her new watercolors for submission in another contest. Her work has matured, and her confidence in that work has increased. Carrie begins to take responsibility for her attempted suicide. She does not wish to hide the truth of her intended overdose. She tells her family that she will not lie, saying that she has bronchitis, if anyone questions her about her absence from school. Carrie's growth also finds her with a newly discovered generosity of spirit. She recognizes that gray exists between the certainties of white and black, and she frees her mother from hewing to her exacting standards. If her mother wants to dismiss Carrie's emotional outburst as separate from her illness and therefore from herself, then Carrie allows her mother that very deception she finds unacceptable for herself. Carrie's truth telling also extends to Daniel, her new next-door neighbor. Their fledgling relationship is built on honesty that includes Daniel's unquestioning knowledge of Carrie's therapy sessions.

Carrie comes to see her connections to others. Her attempted suicide disrupted more lives than just her own. She will never be able to erase Moira's memory of finding her unconscious in the bathroom, but she can apologize to and comfort her sister. Carrie risks feeling close to Moira again. She also begins honestly to express darker emotions. In a fit of anger at learning the truth of rumors surrounding Mrs. Ramsay, Carrie throws a pillow and breaks a lamp. She clears the broken pieces and tells her mother she must be held accountable for this action.

Along with Carrie's self-acceptance, she starts to take risks that previously panicked and overwhelmed her. It becomes Carrie's decision, not her mother's or Moira's, to attend the junior dance. "She knew it was something she needed to do" (*LG,* 156), a fear she needs to overcome, a sign of her wellness, a rite of passage she must complete as a normal adolescent in her community.

Boy-girl friendships are another aspect of adolescent normalcy. Carrie originally shies away from Daniel Spangler, anxious their relationship could develop into one similar to that Moira has with Matt, Daniel's brother. Carrie and Daniel discover common interests as they share with each other their discomfort at the dance.

Oneal highlights Carrie's entrance to adolescence in a scene reminiscent of Katherine Paterson's *Bridge to Terabithia*. As Jess incorporates Leslie's death into his life by sharing the secret place of Terabithia with May Beth, so Carrie lets go of the island of the language of goldfish by sharing it. At the end of summer, Carrie introduces young Sara Myers to the magic of goldfish. Carrie sees her island for what it is: "a pile of rocks in the middle of the pond . . . she could easily reach . . . with the handle of a broom" (*LG*, 179), not a never-ending childhood paradise.

4. Shattering Formality

In Zibby Oneal's second novel, *A Formal Feeling* (1982), 16-year-old Anne Cameron returns home from boarding school for the holiday season. Unlike her roommate and other school friends, she does not anticipate the journey home with jubilant excitement. Anne's controlled anxiety surrounding her homecoming stems from her mother's death and her father's recent remarriage. Anne's visit lives up (or down) to her expectations. The house holds inescapable memories of her mother—from the unused, out-of-tune piano in the living room to the blue-bordered china dinner plates. In the midst of her mother's house and her mother's family, Anne cannot tolerate Dory, her new stepmother, and is especially annoyed by her brother Spencer's unquestioning acceptance of Dory as a family member. Even easy-going Laura, Anne's best friend and the one person she perceived as being constant and consistent, has changed in subtle ways.

Before the story begins, the novel's inherent sense of formality is apparent. The novel borrows its title from the opening line of an Emily Dickinson poem that appears as the frontispiece:

> After great pain, a formal feeling comes—
> The Nerves sit ceremonious, like Tombs—
> The stiff Heart questions was it He, that bore,
> And Yesterday, or Centuries before?

The Feet, mechanical, go round—
A Wooden way
Of Ground, or air, or Ought—
Regardless grown,
A Quartz contentment, like a stone—

This is the Hour of Lead—
Remembered, if outlived,
As Freezing persons, recollect the Snow—
First—Chill—then Stupor—then the letting go—[1]

The poem gives shape and language to the novel, offers clues to Anne's character, and traces her struggle. Oneal incorporates the words and images of the poem into the novel's foundation. "Like most of [Dickinson's other] poems on extreme mental states, this one provides no narrative context, nor does it identify a specific speaker.[2] Oneal's "poet's pen / turns them to shapes, and gives to airy nothing / a local habitation and a name."[3] Anne becomes the poem's speaker; the poem becomes Anne's story. By novel's end, Anne has claimed the poem as her own: "She *knew* the poem. She understood it just as she understood that the trees outside the window were three-dimensional."[4]

The novel reverberates with images of stiffness, stone, and cold. The unrelieved bleakness and cold of winter dominate the action and setting. Like the poem's speaker, Anne, who is "always cold" (*FF*, 12), initially experiences a great pain, which hardens into formality; she "remain[s] enclosed . . . in a shell of crystal" (*FF*, 15). After her mother's abandonment, Anne's heart stiffens and becomes unyielding: "She forecloses the possibility of either knowledge or sensation" (Eberwein, 141). By mistakenly questioning with her heart, Anne cuts herself off from answers only a rational mind can provide. For Anne, time has lost perspective and continuity. Her mother died over a year ago, yet Anne feels her mother's presence everywhere. The fact that the novel is written in the past and past perfect tenses underscores Anne's success in mourning her loss and letting go.

The color blue dominates the visual imagery of *A Formal Feeling*—Anne's blue eyes, the blue of Mrs. Cameron's hyacinths, the blue border of Mrs. Cameron's fine china, the blue music book, the blue rabbit Anne's mother gives her, the blue of Anne's sweater (also a gift from her mother, but one that has remained hidden in a dresser drawer): "Blue. Everything blue. Blue and more blue all her life, because, she had been told, it was a color that looked pretty with her hair, hers and her mother's" (*FF*, 139). This blue is icy cold and deep, not pale or transparent. It chills and permeates the novel, instilling a relentless formality.

Anne's activities help define the narrative shape of the novel. Like the poem's endlessly treading mechanical feet, Anne's two physical activities, running and skating, are essentially circuitous; they begin and end in the same place. Their circularity mimics the novel's shape, which opens with a plane, carrying Anne home, circling the airport, and closes with Anne's returning, again by plane, to school. In between, Anne seems to be getting nowhere, repeating her actions automatically. Her running, her going around, allows a stoppage for her. While running, she concentrates only on movement: "For a mile or so she felt her legs, was aware of her breathing and the pumping of her arms. She heard sounds around her, noticed things. But after two miles it became automatic. Her legs ran out, not because she commanded them, but because they had fallen into the rhythm of running. Sounds and distractions fell away. Gradually she stopped thinking. By the end of the two miles she knew she would be only— mindlessly—running" (*FF*, 14).

Skating, too, provides Anne with escape. On the ice, her activities are directed, circular, and controlled. During her first trip to the pond, Anne practices figure eights with grueling rigidity. During her second trip, Anne again circumscribes the figure eight, and she also rediscovers how to spin, pulling in, turning in rapid, small circles.

In learning to play the piano from her mother, Anne's inability to reproduce the circle of key signs frustrates her. In repeating the exercise in efforts to master it, Anne's fingers "stiffen" and "freeze" (*FF*, 138). She is stymied, unable to free herself from the entrapment of repetition. Anne experiences similar obstructions in her attempts to complete an assignment for a paper about a novel whose central image is circular—a novel in which the character journeys into and out of the heart of darkness. She irregularly picks up and then abandons this work. Anne is locked into a pattern not of writing but of trying to write. As in her piano exercises, she never progresses beyond a beginning.

Even in more cerebral activities, circularity dominates. Anne's memories intrude on her; time is confused as past and present slip in and out of each other. As she skates, writes the paper, or rediscovers favorite books of her childhood, Anne remembers seemingly isolated incidents from her past. Memories of the carousel have particular lucidity. She recalls the palpable anticipation of her annual, end-of-summer carousel ride. As she remembers, Anne re-creates the pleasure and the freedom she experienced in the whirling movement of the carousel.

The dynamic force of Emily Dickinson's poem is created by alternating "images of motion and form and images of immobility and dissolution . . . [and] the basic development of the poem is from potential to kinetic energy."[5] Repeated motifs of spinning and whirling in *A Formal Feeling* stand in dramatic contrast to patterns of stasis. As Anne approaches home, she pictures the house in the idealized completeness of spring, with her mother's magnolias and hyacinths in full bloom. She represses the reality of stark, bare winter and her mother's absence. Unable to face the inevitable clash between fantasy and reality because "things were moving too fast" (*FF*, 8), Anne postpones her arrival home with another drive around the block. Upon her return, Anne expects the house and its contents to be in the same perfect order it was while her mother lived there. Instead, "a scatter of mail—torn envelopes, bills, a schedule of concerts, . . . two dirty coffee cups and the soggy remains of breakfast toast" (*FF*, 8) greet Anne. The heady perfume of the tacky dyed carnations has replaced the "elusive" smell of carefully arranged eucalyptus leaves in her mother's bedroom. Dory's ever-changing disorder and chaos have replaced the fixed perfection of her mother.

Anne attempts to make changes in her home that will ensure its staying the same. Distressed that no one has prepared her mother's rose bushes for the oncoming winter, Anne performs this task and then repairs the clumsy bird feeder her father had built for her mother. In imposing a familiar order, Anne hopes to recapture the feeling of security she remembers from her childhood. When Mrs. Mortimer, Anne's next-door neighbor, shows her a number of photographs of the family, Anne examines them closely, perusing the frozen images. As she looks at the photographs, Anne is "strangely disturbed. In all the pictures they looked so young, so invulnerable, so happy—as if nothing bad could ever touch them" (*FF*, 66). Anne desperately wants to regain that feeling of invincibility.

Like looking at photographs that isolate moments, stopping them in time, Anne frequently looks into the lighted windows of houses she passes by. She has no entry into these idealized scenes of family togetherness. She is on the other side of the glass pane, looking in. As she yearns for the happy family she remembers from her childhood, Anne simultaneously excludes herself from the family she now has. She assigns herself the role of outsider looking in: "It was like watching a play she thought. No more real than that. They were actors putting on a homecoming scene and she was the audience, sitting high up in the second balcony, reluctantly watching the fiction unfold" (*FF*, 24). Anne does not take an active part in the family life; she distances herself and observes.

Even when she is first home alone, Anne does not reclaim the place that was hers or create a new one. Rather, she wanders uncomfortably, ill at ease. As long as she aimlessly walks through the house, Anne can notice but does not need to acknowledge any of the changes. She approaches her parents' bedroom with reluctance. She goes directly to her mother's inherited pier-glass mirror and is unable to escape her own image reflected there. She looks to the mirror to confirm reality; however, "her reflection lay beneath the glass untouched and untouchable" (*FF*, 53). She can only recite the fact of her mother's death to the mirror. The recitation gives the words voice but not body, depth, or meaning. Framing her own reflection, Anne sees her parents' room in the mirror. Even noticing the dangling stocking and the garish carnations, which have replaced her mother's tasteful eucalyptus leaves, evokes no emotional response from Anne.

Anne searches her mirror image for confirmation of a happy childhood spent with devoted parents: "Anne turned . . . to the pier glass hunting reassurance in its speckled surface. But saw only her own unbelieving face" (*FF*, 11). This contradiction forms the base of tension in the novel. Anne remembers a perfect house presided over by a perfect mother. But something unnerves her; a persistent undercurrent ripples her calm surface. She cannot find the words for it; in fact, every time she gets closer to naming the ambivalence, she retreats and then desists. But the memory of some unnamed truth concerning her relationship with her mother comes into sharper focus. Her memory is selective: Anne recalls being angry at her mother for denying permission to ride the carousel more than once a season; another time she remembers excruciating piano practices conducted with exacting standards by her mother; yet another time she relives the endless torture of skating figure eights under her mother's demanding supervision. These isolated, seemingly disconnected memories seem to contain some deeper meaning that Anne fears to confront, and she shelves them into separate compartments. Over time Anne has become a master at forgetting. The vital reason for forgetting is the one thing Anne is unable to remember. Ambivalence, doubt, and complication characterize Anne's relationship with her mother. Theirs was not the perfect relationship she would prefer to remember.

How does Anne move beyond denial to a truthful understanding of her relationship with her mother? The activities in which Anne engages promote her denial. When the truth surfaces or gets close enough to be uncomfortable, Anne literally runs away from it. Her mobility provides her escape; as long as her body is active, she need not think about unpleasantness. Only when Anne stops moving do the separate pieces of her relationship with her mother begin to form a whole picture. While skating, Anne "[catches] an edge" (*FF*, 18), falls, and injures her ankle. Her recovery imposes immobility. She can flee the truth no longer; it has caught up with her. Moments after the fall, "she sat staring blankly at her foot, but it was not her foot she saw. With a clarity that astonished her, she saw something else—a child sitting upright in a train" (*FF,* 144). It is that child, her eight-year-old self, whose existence Anne has denied.

Anne has been unable to integrate the eight-year-old's feelings of abandonment, anger, and anxiety caused by her mother with the 16-year-old's regulated self-composure. Her mother's death causes a second abandonment, this one at age 16, even though Anne has repressed the first. The child Anne believes she is the cause when her mother leaves the family to live by herself. Frustrated at her inability to perform a piano piece to her mother's satisfaction, young Anne openly vents her anger and silently wishes her mother to disappear. When her wishes become reality and her mother does leave, Anne holds herself responsible. From that day on, Anne refuses to feel. She becomes cold, removed, formal. She retreats into a self-created "shell of crystal" (*FF,* 15). Anne also believes she is the reason for her mother's return. Anne perceives that her diligent practice with the skates her mother sent her, her refusal to cry when she falls on the ice, and her ultimate repression of all emotion were the reasons for her mother's return. Anne's eight-year-old logic burdens her with the responsibility for her mother's disappearance and also for her mother's reappearance. Anne manages this burden effectively for eight years by forgetting her abandonment and her feelings because of it. At 16, Anne has become her mother's daughter in all respects. Like her mother, Anne is controlled and controlling, remote and emotionless, demanding and unresponsive.

When the doctor tells Anne that there are some things over which she does not have control, such as the time needed to heal her sprained ankle, Anne is both surprised and liberated. She refuses the prescribed painkillers; she allows the pain to wash over her—both the literal pain of her injured ankle and the remembered pain of her mother's abandonment. "Whenever she woke, she felt the ache of her ankle and the ache of the memory as if they were one—quiet, steady aches that would heal if she let them" (*FF*, 21). Remembering the difficult past frees Anne from its bondage.

Remembering also demands that Anne question her relationship with her mother: "If she loved me, why did she leave me? Beneath it there was another . . . she knew the question had always been there, unspeakable, at the bottom of all she remembered and had chosen to forget and she made herself ask: Did I ever love my mother at all?" (*FF*, 155). The answers enable Anne to see her mother as imperfect, a recognition that permits Anne to be imperfect also.

Prior to this epiphany, all of Anne's relationships were colored by her connection to her mother. She held other people to the same exacting standards that characterized her relationship with her mother. From the start, her father's new wife, Dory, cannot compete with Anne's memory of her perfect mother and falls victim to Anne's disdain and abuse. A sloppy housekeeper, clumsy, and brimming with childlike enthusiasm, Dory's generous nature embraces Anne, but Anne rejects Dory and her warm overtures. When Anne confesses to Dory in a panic that she accidentally broke one of her mother's cherished china-blue hyacinth plates, Anne is grateful for her stepmother's easy forgiveness. Unlike Anne's mother, Dory dismisses the damage as only a plate, not a bone, not a person who had been broken. As Anne assimilates new knowledge about her mother, she begins to permit Dory's comfort and support. As the novel progresses, Anne accepts Dory as her father's wife, the new Mrs. Cameron. At the novel's conclusion, Anne selects a photograph of her father as a young man for Dory's Christmas present. In sharing the photograph, Anne delights in Dory's pleasure. She has come to accept Dory as she has come to accept her mother: an imperfect person whom she can love. She can imagine reaching out to touch Dory's hand rather than pulling back from her mother's hands.

At first, Anne views her parents as a unit. She assumes their actions and decisions represent mutual desires. To Anne, they are not individuals but are bound as one. As in *The Language of Goldfish,* Oneal gives neither parent a first name. Their roles as parents define their identity. As Anne separates herself from her mother, she also separates her father from her mother. During her visit home, Anne detects her mother's presence everywhere. Her mother dominated everything from Anne's thoughts to the selection of the family car, the choice of china dinner plates and the family's decision about a Christmas tree. Like the moody adolescent Hamlet, who has suffered a parental loss, Anne too bemoans and sits in judgment of her father's hasty marriage to a mate she deems less worthy. But as Anne struggles with the burden of memories about her mother, she also faces new information about her father. Her mother may have liked the family car, but her father did not. Her mother may have wanted a Christmas tree proportionate to the size of the room, but her father always wanted bigger trees, "hotel lobby trees" (*FF,* 72) that filled the space. Her mother may have carefully tended the rose bushes and garden, but her father builds only a clumsy, awkward bird feeder that is in constant need of repair. Anne begins to see her father as an independent person with his own needs and desires, as someone who would want and need to marry a woman unlike her mother, a woman like Dory.

Her older brother, Spencer, sympathizes with the void Anne feels at her mother's absence. Wanting to make her return home more comfortable, he picks her up at the airport and agrees to spend more time at home than he had planned. Spencer may detect Anne's difficulties, but he has no real sense of the depth of Anne's repression about her mother. Anne denies him entry to her world; she refuses to discuss her feelings with him. No matter how much Spencer worries about Anne, she distances herself from him:

> "You know what, Anne? It's like you're surrounded by a moat."
> She shoved her half-empty bowl to one side. "Spoken like a true medievalist's son," she said.
> "See what I mean. I can't get to you."
> Anne picked up a breadstick and began crumbling it on the table. "Did it ever occur to you that maybe I don't want to be got to?" (*FF,* 61).

Spencer's honest memories of a less-than-perfect mother threaten Anne's self-protective idealization of her mother. As Anne moves toward a realistic acceptance of her mother, her relationship with Spencer loses its formal edge. On her final day at home, Spencer finds Anne in the attic, mourning her mother. Anne quietly welcomes the comfort and support he offers.

The DeWitts, the family of Anne's best friend, Laura, stand in dramatic contrast to Anne's formal family. Laura and her entire family are casual and emotive in ways Anne does not see at home and in ways contrary to her personality. This trait appeals to Anne even as it unnerves her. On a walk to choir practice, Oneal characterizes the basic difference between Anne and Laura as they disagree about the choir's ability to meet the choirmaster's expectation:

> "He just wants it to be good," [Anne] said.
> "No. He wants it to be perfect."
> "So?"
> "So that's unrealistic, given us." (*FF*, 113)

Anne must let go of her obsession with perfection. Laura's easygoing manner and accepting family help Anne by example.

When Anne is not alone, she spends time with Laura. During Anne's visit home Laura involves her in the choir; they go gift shopping together, and Anne relaxes at Laura's house. Even when the two young women are most comfortable with each other— talking about school, common friends, and boys—Anne is unable to free herself completely from her crystal shell. Laura confides her disappointment and unhappiness at not being asked to a dance. While Anne's tendency is to shrug off these feelings and to move on, Laura makes no effort to hide her tears. In response, Anne does not reach out to her friend to offer consolation and comfort; rather, she demands that Laura control her emotions and stop crying. Anne insists that Laura "not mind . . . That's the only way. You can't let yourself mind things" (*FF*, 81). This blatant, free display of emotion frightens Anne. Just after her mother's death, Anne goes to the attic, and, embracing her mother's clothing, she painfully sobs, "ripped with feeling she couldn't even explain" (*FF*, 56). Her own outburst frightens her in its intensity and inexplicability. Anne promises herself she will never indulge in it again. Anne holds true to this promise, denying herself and others the freedom to cry, until the novel's close when she comes to accept her mother's imperfections. She deliberately returns to the attic, again embraces her mother's clothing, "and knew deeply and for the first time that her mother was dead. She put her face against the soft velvet as if it were a shoulder. And then she wept, weeping for her mother, telling her good-bye" (*FF*, 161). In experiencing this farewell, Anne becomes more accepting of her own emotions and may begin to allow Laura and others their own emotional expression.

Anne has spent part of her time at home avoiding her feelings in general, but especially avoiding her feelings about Eric, her boyfriend from last summer. Toward the end of the summer, in August, Anne had begun to separate from Eric, repressing her feelings for him. At school she barely remembered him as a person. For a while she remembered the smell of his hair; eventually she only remembered remembering (*FF*, 47). Anne's relationship with her mother is a primary source for the apparent shift in Anne's perception of Eric. Anne's mother has been dead nearly a year when in August her father begins to seek Dory's company with frequency. Anne perceives Dory as intrusive; Dory threatens to replace her mother as her father's wife. Subconsciously Anne worries that Dory the living person will overshadow the memory of her mother, a memory Anne is compelled to keep alive. Anne also perceives Dory as a personal threat. In the past, Anne and her father had spent summer evenings reading Dante's *Divine Comedy;* Mr. Cameron may now choose to spend time with Dory rather than with Anne. Although Anne may have elected to go out with Eric and not stay home with her father on any given evening, Dory threatens Anne's control of her time with her father. Anne responds by repressing her feelings for Eric to enable herself to separate from him.

August also signals Anne's imminent return to school. Anne begins this inevitable separation from Eric early. Originally she had not wanted to return to school. One can speculate on her reasons for wanting to stay at home: to be with Eric or to protect her father, and her home, from Dory's invasion. In either case, Anne thinks her father, like her mother before him, wants her to go away to school. Like her mother's previous abandonments, Anne's father now distances himself from her and forces her to go alone: "Sometime in August winter had begun again" (*FF,* 30). Anne turns inward, cuts off her feelings, and returns to school. She denies herself any memories of the summer, even the pleasant ones of kissing Eric and reading aloud on the porch with her father. Anne's fear of abandonment, originally stemming from her mother's abandonment of her, refuses acknowledgment of any feelings. Anne's catharsis in the attic renews her emotional life. While she has spent her time at home avoiding Eric, as she boards the plane to return to school Anne considers writing to Eric, willing to risk emotional involvement.

5. Painting Summer's Light

Home from boarding school on summer vacation and recuperating from mononucleosis, 17-year-old Kate Brewer of *In Summer Light* (1985) finds herself bored, restless, and resentful. Her father, the famous painter Marcus Brewer, is a dominant presence in the family's home off the coast of Massachusetts. As in *The Language of Goldfish,* the island setting plays an integral role in this novel. Ian Jackson, an attractive graduate student from California, brings a welcome disruption to Kate's days when he arrives to catalog her father's paintings. With Ian's gentle friendship and her mother's quiet support, Kate begins not only to reevaluate her father as more than a demanding and difficult person but also to rediscover her own talents and aspirations. Kate's is a summer of healing and of growth.

Painterly images dominate the novel from its opening, as in *The Language of Goldfish.* The readers' perceptions are filtered through the eyes of a main character who is an artist. Unlike Carrie, who has begun to discover the artistic possibilities of color, Kate has consciously repressed her talent and her desire to be a painter, yet she perceives her world with the visual sensitivity of an artist. Despite the novel's third-person narration, the reader's introduction to the Brewer's home is shaped by Kate's artistic vision. Her friend Leah sees the painting over the mantelpiece as a portrait of Kate as a child, but Oneal describes the painting through Kate herself as simply a study of light: "There were peaches in a blue and white Chinese bowl and a cat almost the color of peaches stretched beneath the table. Morning light fell slantwise across the table's surface, lay like marmalade on the rungs of a ladder-back chair. Beside the table, sitting straight on the straight-backed chair, was a little girl, feet bare, hands folded" (*ISL,* 3). Slowly Oneal enlarges the scene, moving away from the close-up focus on the painting of 10-year-old Kate to include the real-life 17-year-old Kate. From the first page, art and life are side by side, a juxtaposition that infuses the novel.

With her artistic lens, Kate isolates moments, framing them. As she looks away from the painting into the kitchen and sees her mother creating a flower arrangement in a Chinese bowl, the image of the bowl Kate sees filled with peaches in the painting and the bowl filled with similarly colored nasturtiums again juxtaposes reality and artifice. As she places the newly filled bowl beneath the painting, Mrs. Brewer's activity is intentionally an act of imitation meant to please Marcus Brewer with her actual mimicry of his artistic creation.

Early in the novel, Oneal reveals the extent of Kate's artistic vision. In looking at the painting, Kate does not see merely a dark-haired girl sitting on a chair in the sun. Rather, Kate perceives the artist's solution of the problem of light. She is aware of the shapes that compose the girl, "whose dark hair grazed the sharp bones of her shoulders" (*ISL,* 3). Kate's annoyance at her mother's attempt to mimic art in life stems in part from her acute sense of color. The nasturtiums and peaches are not the same color: "the pale gold in the skin of the peach, a suggestion of the flesh beneath, . . . was entirely lacking in the flowers" (*ISL,* 5). Later, when Kate looks at her mother cooking in the kitchen, she sees a figure, a design, and a pattern: "the green of her mother's skirt, the curve of her arm, the copper, the white froth of the eggs" (*ISL,* 96).

Despite her artist's intuition, Kate rejects painting. In a discussion with Ian, Kate admits to noticing color but quickly asserts that she does not consciously think about it. She refuses to be another artist in her family; one, she insists, is enough. Now a senior at boarding school, Kate has already declared her intent to major in English, not art, at college. Her half of her room at school, unlike her room at home and unlike her father's studio, is celllike, sparse, and monotone. Kate represses her artistic tendencies to the extreme of absenting color totally from the space she alone controls. She does not deny her talent, but she does prohibit its expression. The prize-winning painting she did as a high school freshman is now wrapped in towels and hidden in back of her closet. She refuses to discuss it as a work—or as indicative of her talent—with her mother. Kate does not want to paint or to remember a time when she did paint.

Painting has been a source of both pleasure and pain for Kate. As a child, she spent time with her father in his studio, painting her pictures as he worked on his. They took trips together to the museum to study the work of other artists. One of her early oil paintings, done from memory, of the island meadow, challenged her and rewarded her with a blue ribbon. But painting also caused Kate pain. At 17, she may understand intellectually her father's painting for which she modeled as a study of morning light in the studio, but emotionally 10-year-old Kate is disappointed and saddened that the painting is not named after her, is not a portrait of her. The 17-year-old Kate remains angry, unable to forget that hurt or to forgive her father for causing it. Her anger deepens when her father dismisses her prize-winning oil painting as "a nice little picture" (*ISL,* 67). When she brings her father coffee one morning, Kate feels in competition with the painting on the easel for his attention. Unable to receive his approval or even his attention, as a father and as an artist, Kate rejects painting—and ultimately rejects her father.

Kate dreads the time she will spend on the island to recuperate. Her father's controlling schedule, moodiness, and general presence dominate the place, and Kate feels unable to escape. He even impedes her ability to complete a paper on Shakespeare's *The Tempest* for English. As she attempts to write about the character of the magician Prospero, her fury at her father colors her view. Kate sees her father as a magician like Prospero—a genius to whom too many allowances have been granted, for whom too many sacrifices have been made.

When Leah, Kate's good friend and roommate from school, visits the family during the summer, she sees instead the charming, magical Marcus Brewer. Kate resents her father's ability to transform himself into someone delightful and enchanting for Leah, a virtual outsider. His sudden charm irks Kate who, as a child, saw her father as a Prince Charming, and stayed up late watching for his studio lights to go out, falling asleep straining to hear his footfalls approach, waiting for a goodnight kiss. Now Marcus Brewer does not seem to be the father Kate wants him to be.

Similarly, Kate struggles with trying to become the daughter Marcus Brewer wants, the daughter to whom Marcus Brewer can be affectionate and enchanting. Initially Kate paints to please her father. Pleasing him is also Kate's reason for ceasing to paint. When he sees her oil painting of the meadow, Marcus Brewer does not feel the pride and joy in her accomplishment Kate expected. Rather, his expression was so peculiar words could not describe it. Her father then banishes Kate from his studio, saying it is too crowded and suggesting she find another place to work. Kate's painting is evidence of her undeniable talent as an artist. The seriousness of it and her obvious talent make her more than Marcus Brewer's daughter; they make her the next painter from the Brewer family. Kate's father's actions reveal his perception of Kate as a threat, a formidable competitor. While he encourages her to find the time and space to pursue her work, he does not comprehend her need to have his approval. He acts like an egotistical artist, not the sympathetic, doting, encouraging father Kate wants him to be.

In her complex, difficult relationship with her father, Kate is faced with a number of options. She could hold to her ideals of a father-daughter relationship. She has tried changing, suppressing her talents and desire to paint in order to remove herself from competition with her father. However, that has not produced the results she expected. With the subtle help of her mother and Ian, Kate arrives at her solution; she comes to an understanding of who her father truly is. Kate recognizes her father as an artist battling his canvas, refusing to give in, refusing to give up his struggle for expression. Further, when Kate impetuously gives her father advice about a painting with which he is experiencing difficulty—telling him not to add the vertical red stroke, for it would worsen the painting—she begins to comprehend the desperation he feels. In an uncharacteristic moment of self-doubt, Marcus Brewer confides in Kate his fear that his ideas have been depleted and his ambivalence at the dubious honor of a retrospective exhibit, suggesting that his best work has been done. This confession marks a turning point in Kate's assessment of her father. Her father becomes unmasked and reveals himself as an old man; human, not evil; not a magician; not her Prince Charming.

Kate's conclusion to her paper about Prospero demonstrates the extent of her reconciliation with her father. While she sees the sacrifices he has demanded of his family as unforgivable, she realizes that she must forgive him nonetheless. Not to forgive him would deprive Kate of the very humanity she finds so lacking in him. Unforgiveness would trap Kate in exactly the same way she finds her father limited—and trapped, as Prospero, on his egotistical island of self-created illusions.

Accepting her father as no more than a man, a man struggling for self-expression in his work, frees Kate. She no longer needs to follow in her father's path; she need not paint in the same way or become the same kind of artist he is. And it removes her from competition with her father, allowing her to develop her own personal style of painting. Despite her respect for her father's work and her recognition of his genius as an artist, Kate dislikes his style. Where he paints the study of morning light in the studio, she would paint a little girl sitting on a chair. Where he depicts the wall of the house abstractly in a harsh vertical stroke, she would represent the wall in recognizable terms, articulating the familiar. Where he is too great, too important a painter to be bothered with doing a child's portrait for an indulgent mother, Kate uses the opportunity to develop her technical skills, to experiment with technique, and to express humanity in her art. An accusation that Kate is as self-absorbed as Marcus propels her to take up her brush and prove her unique way of painting.

When Kate remembers the summer, she remembers the quiet time during August, a time created by Ian, and she remembers the peace of working with her mother in the garden. Ian Jackson and Floss Brewer, Kate's mother, quietly guide her to a new understanding of her father and, simultaneously, direct her return to art.

When Ian first arrives in his unimpressive old car and drenched yellow slicker, Kate assesses him as a courteous and awed admirer of her father. She expects Ian to fall into the standard behavior exhibited by her father's other followers: subservient, remote, and deferential. Feeling so hurt by her father, Kate is wary of a stranger. Ian's engaging personality and genuine attentiveness cause Kate to reevaluate her initial prejudgment of him. At Marcus Brewer's direction, Kate shows Ian around their land and brings him to the studio backroom where he will stay as he catalogs Brewer's paintings for the upcoming retrospective.

On this tour, Kate finds Ian to be a careful, generous listener. He is easy to talk to and comfortable to be with. As they talk, Ian notices Kate's artist's perspective and way of describing her world. He wonders why Kate, who has such a fine sense of color, is not a painter, and he comprehends immediately what Kate has struggled to make her mother understand: she needs to discover her own path, make her own contributions to the world, go where no one else in her family has been. In choosing to be an English major, she intentionally rejects the paths her parents have taken and embarks on a new road, one all her own and removed from her father's shadow.

The friendship between Kate and Ian slowly develops and intensifies. He works diligently on his cataloging, but he also makes time to relax. Kate too tries to work on her paper about *The Tempest,* and she welcomes Ian's company as she relaxes. Ian's inquisitiveness about Kate transcends an academic curiosity about the artist's daughter. His genuine interest in her as a person allows her to share with him and also invites her reciprocal curiosity. Their friendship becomes mutual and trusting.

The integrity of their friendship allows Kate to let down her guard. Ian's questions awaken dormant feelings in Kate as they make her think about difficult topics. His curiosity about Kate's decision not to paint causes her to ask the same question of herself and to reconsider. When Ian shares his need to risk anything for his brother's approval, Kate painfully recognizes her own willingness to do anything to gain her father's affection. As he shares the futility and frustration of those attempts, Kate begins to feel the hurt of her own fruitless outreaches to her father.

Kate's level of emotional comfort with Ian is so strong that she takes him into her confidence and risks sharing secrets that expose her unconscious feelings. She recounts to Ian a particularly memorable trip as a child to the museum with her father where they view a Monet painting of a poppy field. She recalls feeling silly for having seen a rabbit hiding in the field and attributes the source of this feeling to her father. Despite his art history training and his definitive knowledge that Monet did not paint a rabbit into the field's landscape, Ian does not pass judgment on her child imagination. He does not condemn her response as foolish; rather, he allows room for her imagination and suggests that everyone is entitled to her own response to art. During another scholar's visit to Kate's father, Ian defends Marcus Brewer's importance as a painter and his rightness in protecting himself and his energies from external, nonpainting demands. The depth of Kate's comfort with Ian unequivocally reveals itself when she retorts, "Well, then, maybe great painters shouldn't have families" (*ISL,* 75). This response is automatic, almost unconscious. Despite her initial desire to reclaim the words because they could adversely influence her relationship with Ian, the comment exhibits Kate's openness with him as she voices her sense that she is burdensome to her father and his work and that he is ineffective as a family man.

Perhaps the most dangerous risk Kate takes with Ian is to paint the cliff she used to paint as a child. Painting the rocks with red clay consumes Kate's energy and attention. As she paints, Kate experiences the same joy and carefreeness she felt as a child and risks rediscovering the deep pleasure and satisfaction of painting. The task absorbs and exhilarates her. As she finishes, Kate jumps off the rock in a "pure feeling of joy, as she sailed through the air, her body like an extension of the curves she had

painted" (*ISL*, 92). Also, Kate risks experiencing again the physical work of painting that involves her entire body; the red clay
ruins her bathing suit. The rock becomes an artistic problem of
shape; the clay is transformed into paint; her hands function as
painter's brushes.

On another day, as they search the attic for the Marcus Brewer
drawings Ian needs for his cataloging notes, Ian and Kate stum-
ble on her mother's last painting, wrapped up and hidden. It
prompts Ian to inquire about Kate's painting. Ambivalent about
showing it to him, she risks his dislike of the painting and shows
it to him. His immediate, honest, and careful praise spark again
Kate's desire to paint. His reaction echoes Mrs. Ramsay's excitement when Carrie begins to experiment with watercolors and
painting the island in *The Language of Goldfish*. With Ian, Kate
is free to remember her childhood and its pains, to recognize the
hard work of painting, and to express her own hidden desires.

Kate's relationship with Ian has created in her a new willingness to be intimate. Oneal's skill as a writer allows readers to
recognize that Kate has fallen in love with Ian long before Kate
herself knows. A careful reading of the novel reveals that Kate
begins to laugh more as she spends time with Ian. It is not forced
or false but the laughter of someone closed now opening up; it is
the laughter of happiness. Early in the novel, Oneal describes
objects from Kate's artistic perspective. Later, in a subtle shift,
Kate begins to see through Ian's eyes. She thinks she knows Ian
well enough to understand what will amuse him and pays attention to things that would bring Ian pleasure or delight. Gradually
Kate's attention is more directed, and she looks at Ian deliberately, intently: "She learned him in the way she had once learned
the meadow, in the smallest, most particular detail—the frayed
edge of his shirtsleeve, the crease of his elbow, the squinting lines
at the corners of his eyes" (*ISL*, 116–17). Kate studies Ian as an
artist studies her subject. Eventually Kate identifies her feelings
for Ian as love.

The depth of her love empowers Kate to take yet another risk:
she asks Ian to take her with him on his upcoming trip to Boston.
This direct statement encompasses meanings beyond the super-

ficial request. In it Kate tells Ian that she loves him and wants to be with him. No longer an immature child, this stronger, more independent Kate loves a man other than her father for the first time. For the moment, Kate overcomes some of the insecurities about love and caring caused by her father.

Unlike the other risks Kate has mastered, this one proves temporarily insurmountable: "Everything she needed to know was written there where nothing was written. It was as if she had entered into a bad old dream" (*ISL*, 123). Kate is once again disappointed, once again let down, once again hurt by the most important man in her life—this time, Ian.

Just as Oneal reveals Kate's developing love for Ian, she unfolds Ian's feelings for Kate deliberately. Unlike Kate, he does not intentionally seek time for them to be alone. He welcomes Kate's sister, Amanda, and her friend Frances on their journeys to the beach. From the very beginning of their relationship, Kate reminds Ian of his sister, and he adopts a brotherly role with her. Like his sister who needed to be encouraged to ride a wagon down the hill, Ian provides encouraging support to Kate as she recovers from mononucleosis, reaches a new understanding of her father, and rediscovers her own painterly talents. Clearly, taking Kate with him to Boston would be inappropriate given his perception of their relationship. His reason for going to Boston is the same as that for being on the island: to continue his work for Marcus Brewer. Ian does not love Kate. His actions and words to her demonstrate, however, that he does care about her. When he is in Boston, he buys her a postcard of the Monet painting they had discussed earlier. Upon his return to the island, he tells her that the time and the circumstances are not right for their romantic involvement. Ian's obvious affection for Kate and his clear unwillingness to inflict pain on her heal the hurt she feels at his rejection. Unlike her father, his concern is for her. He shares his thoughts without the intrusion of a proud ego. He honestly tells Kate the truth about his feelings with respect for her dignity and integrity.

Kate's mother has a generosity of spirit similar to Ian's. Like Ian, Floss Brewer truly recognizes her husband's genius. She en-

gineers the environment not only to support his work and schedule but also to please him. Like Ian, her work quietly creates
order. Also like Ian, Floss Brewer perceives Kate's talent and repressed desire to become an artist.

Floss and Kate enjoy a strong, open relationship. Clearly Kate's
decision to be an English major has been a topic of debate between mother and daughter. Floss wants Kate to become an artist. In Kate she sees the artistic gifts she lacked and does not
want them wasted. Floss continually encourages Kate to direct
her talent and to pursue her art. From the time Kate was a young
child, Floss nurtured Kate's artistic interests. As Kate learns in
the novel's conclusion, it was her mother, not her father, who sent
Kate on trips to the museum with Marcus, and it was her mother
who bought Kate her first set of paints. This knowledge further
releases Kate's sense of debt to her father as it establishes a
strong mother-daughter bond and deepens Floss's understanding
of the importance of painting to Kate.

An active area of controversy between Kate and her mother is
Floss's decision, made over 20 years ago, to stop painting seriously. Kate wrongly interprets this decision as one made in deference to Marcus Brewer. He could not live in a house in which
he was not the only painter, where he was not the primary focus
of attention. Kate truly believes her mother has more talent than
she admits to. Because of this misconception of her mother's reasons for relegating her painting to the attic, Kate's intolerance
and resentment of her father grow. Kate unjustly assumes the
responsibility for fighting this nonexistent battle. She is outraged
that her mother spends time and effort to create an environment
pleasing to Marcus Brewer. "She gave as much care to arranging
[day lilies] as she might have given to a permanent work of art.
And why? Because Kate's father liked them" (*ISL*, 128–29). Misunderstanding her mother's motives, Kate unfairly passes judgment about the activities in which her mother does engage. She
finds her mother overqualified to teach art to children and to
paint a wall mural in Amanda's room. She sees the work as su-
perficial and demeaning, a waste of the talent she is sure her
mother has. Despite Kate's sensitivity to and appreciation of her

mother's hard work in the garden, using it as a kind of canvas, she still feels her mother deprives herself of a greater calling.

In many ways, Kate projects onto her mother the ambition to paint that she denies herself. She continually assumes her mother had the same choice that she, Kate, could have: to become a master painter or to be a loving and supportive wife and mother. It is not until Kate, with Ian, unwraps her mother's painting, seeing it as it really is—not as she remembered and imagined it to be—that Kate accepts the absence of choice. Her mother does not have the talent necessary to achieve greatness; she does not possess the genius of Marcus Brewer. When Kate begins to re-learn drawing and painting under her mother's tutelage, Kate realizes that one could learn the technical, mechanical aspects of art but "it was the other thing that you couldn't learn, it was simply there, like a present. She knew because she recognized this other thing in her father's work" (*ISL,* 136).

Even if Kate believes that all her mother's choices were secondary to Marcus Brewer's needs and made in deference to him, her mother's actions also nourish Kate as a daughter. She welcomes Leah to the island for a weekend visit, though it might prove disruptive to Marcus Brewer, because she recognizes Kate's need to see Leah. Floss notices Kate's intensifying affection for Ian. Not wanting Kate to be hurt, she frets about it and discusses her worry with her daughter. When Ian departs, her mother perceives the loss Kate is feeling and comforts her quietly: "They sat at the kitchen table, drinking coffee, and they didn't talk at all. Then her mother took her hand and held it, as she sometimes had done when Kate was a child" (*ISL,* 131).

Both her seven-year-old sister, Amanda and, her roommate and friend, Leah, contribute valuable insights to Kate's personality. In many ways, each exhibits attributes that are opposite those of Kate. As Kate watches Amanda and their father, she is struck by Amanda's casual ease with him. She has never been unself-conscious enough to cuddle up to him, to seek his affection openly the way Amanda can. Like Anne Cameron in *A Formal Feeling,* Kate's sense of formality and reserve intrudes. Her very strength as a painter sharpens her awareness. Despite Kate's unspoken wish to have an intimate, uncomplicated relationship with her father, her analytic nature makes her extremely aware of and especially sensitive to their uncomfortable interaction. She does not acknowledge the basic differences between Amanda's bouncy personality and her own more serious one. Yet these differences play a key role in Marcus Brewer's responses to his two daughters.

Perhaps the 10-year age difference between Amanda and Kate nearly eliminates the potential for their rivalry as siblings. The two seem in competition only with Ian. While Amanda clearly likes Ian, and he her, and she wants to be taken on trips to the beach and to the fireworks, Kate resents Amanda's tagging along. Kate wants to spend time alone with Ian as their relationship deepens. Conversely, like any other young child, Amanda simply wants to be included and charmingly considers herself the center of everyone's attention.

Leah too exhibits a winning freshness, a breathlessness and transparency that appeal to Kate even as these qualities contrast with her own personality. In their conversations about Prospero, Leah accepts the character at face value. Kate, on the other hand, examines and scrutinizes everything and everyone. Leah's sense of humor charms other people and relaxes her companions. In her own self-assessment, Kate is formal, not easy, with other people. Leah wants everyone, especially Kate, to be happy. Her cheery outlook and genuine enthusiasm for life and for other people make her an optimist and a good friend for Kate. After Leah's weekend visit, when Kate confides the truth about why she has stopped painting, Leah has two reactions. First, she confronts Kate with the ridiculousness of the reason. According to Leah's common sense, Kate's talent and clear need to paint should inform her decision, not the lack of praise from her self-absorbed father. Second, in her future correspondence with Kate, Leah continues to offer funny stories about the oddities of fathers, stories that are meant to console Kate. A good listener, Leah detects the burden Kate bears because of her father. A good friend, Leah treats the issue seriously and remains sensitive and supportive.

As she does with Amanda, Kate observes the effortlessness of Leah's rapport with Marcus Brewer and feels excluded—a witness to Marcus Brewer's creation of a magical event, not a participant in it. Kate is hungry for the attention Marcus Brewer gives so easily to Leah and Amanda.

Once again Zibby Oneal captures the thematic essence of the novel in her title. *In Summer Light* provides both a focal point and a rich metaphor for the novel. *In Summer Light* transcends its limited interpretation as only temporal setting. It suggests the novel's aura of warmth, romance, and impressionistic color. As she moves out of the shadow cast by her father, Kate moves into the shadowless brilliance and intensity of summer's light, where she discovers the clarity and distinction of her own form as an artist and as a person. In the novel's opening pages, in which Kate looks at a painting of herself as a child, she sees only a figure, a shape, just as a person standing in the direct light of the sun would be seen by an oncomer only as a figure. As the on-comer moves closer, the figure takes on specific features and recognizable characteristics. So too does Kate fill in her own form with unique features and individuality, increasingly completing herself as the novel progresses.

6. Awakenings

We all harbor fantasies of being the unlucky lucky child, abandoned at birth, left on the forgotten doorstep of some decent, common, poor folk. We alone suspect the truth about our ancestral heritage. We alone believe that we are truly the lost heir to the kingdom, waiting to come of age and discover the courage and power to assume our rightful place as ruler of the land. While many of us merely indulge this fantasy in the lonely recesses of our imagination, a few talented individuals develop the fantasy as they weave words into a magical, encompassing web of fiction. Zibby Oneal is one such artist. Her books are a tapestry of contemporary stories constructed from the fabric of childhood fears, yearnings, and imagination bound together with the threads of recognized childhood fairy tales.

"A writer is like a kaleidoscope filled with colored glass. Shift and the pattern shifts, . . . the pieces tumble and reassemble. But they are the same pieces."[1] This notion of metamorphosis permeates Oneal's work. She tells and retells the stories she made up during her childhood. Similarly, her rich literary heritage provides her with classic tales for modern retellings.

Zibby Oneal recalls telling herself stories from a young age. She remembers a story she created when she was somewhere between four and six years old under the shade of an old elm tree. In it, dapper Mr. Cutting, dressed in tux and tails and boasting a fragrant red rose in his buttonhole, danced his way into her heart. As she grew older and her infant sister demanded more space, causing the family to move, the elm tree was replaced by a fishpond bordering on the new back yard, and the child-storyteller dressed Mr. Cutting in pirate's garb. While Mr. Cutting was purely an imaginary figure, Scarface the Pirate, a spent match found in the grass near the pond, takes on a physical reality. In the storyteller's words, "Scarface cruised the pond in a walnut shell, his job being to guard the beautiful princess who lived in lonely splendor on the rocky island at its center. This he did, and he did it admirably, though he rarely spoke. . . . He had a single line as I recall, and it was this: 'Nobody,' he'd say in a fine gruff tone, 'Nobody may disturb the beautiful princess on the rocky island. She is my *only* daughter'" ("Metamorphosis," 5). Like Carrie, the prepubescent Zibby Oneal began to outgrow the pond, its island, pirate, and princess but did not let go of the story. Scarface was transformed into a trumpeter and the princess into a figure skater. They entertained the war troops and held performances, sharing their special magic around the world.

This young child created these stories from her heart, letting them speak the longings she felt deeply. Mr. Cutting, Scarface the matchstick pirate, and the enchanting trumpeter embodied her need for a romantic hero. They were trustworthy and reliable in ways that adults living in a real world may not be. The heroes' partners filled the young storyteller's need to be at the center of the story. They bask in their "magnificent onliness" ("Metamorphosis," 5) carefree and not burdened like real children with friends, parents, and siblings.

In these early fictional creations, character plays a primary, if not solitary, role. Plot is limited, setting inconsequential, and theme barely realized. As the interview opening this book reveals, character remained primary for the grown author Zibby Oneal. She recalls her first encounter with Carrie:

> One day some years ago I was working in my garden, staking
> the few delphinium that had agreed to bloom that rainy sum-

mer. I was fully occupied with my stakes and twine and hardly
noticed at first that a skinny, lonely, troubled thirteen-year-old
was trying to attract my attention. Yet there she was, impa-
tient to be noticed, and it became clear that she planned to stay
right where she was until I was willing to give her my full re-
gard. Which I certainly was not prepared to do. She looked too
familiar. She looked like someone I'd known once.

It is often true for me that this is how characters show up—
uninvited guests who hang around the edges of my mind until
I'm willing to notice them. Like uninvited guests, they are en-
dured, but not necessarily embraced. So, too, with this imagined girl, this fantasy child. I gave her the spare room in my
head, but I wasn't about to make her pancakes. Yet there was
something about her. . . . Partly it was her persistence, her
downright doggedness. She wouldn't leave me alone. Pretty
soon her stuff was strewn all over the place. She had taken over
the house. It seemed she had some place she wanted to go,
some place she was insisting on taking me. And finally, in ex-
asperation, looking for a little peace and quiet, I followed her.
("Metamorphosis," 7–8)

Now the characters have a story to tell—the story of their metamorphosis, their release from the cocoon of childhood and flight
into an adult world. How different are these stories about 13-
year-old Carrie, 16-year-old Anne, and 17-year-old Kate from
their predecessors about the dancer and her partner Mr. Cutting,
the island princess and her pirate defender Scarface, and the figure skater and her magical trumpeter? Not very different, after
all. Oneal attributes the sameness of the recurring patterns to
"unfinished business" ("Metamorphosis," 8)—the unfinished
business that inevitably takes one back to one's own childhood
and to the tensions and difficulties inherent in the parent-child
relationship.

Oneal's gift allows her to transcend the specificity of her own
experience to express its universality through imaginative recon-
struction and artful crafting. In *The Language of Goldfish*, readers recognize Carrie as the child whose familiar and safe
residence has been shattered by a geographic move. Like many
other children (and like the author who moved as a young child),
Carrie feels misplaced and fractured. For Carrie, Oneal reinvents

the goldfish pond from her own "new" back yard. Oneal's Scarface the Pirate may not patrol the island's borders, but, like the child Oneal was—like any other child—Carrie fantasizes about being the solitary princess yearning for protection from the outside world.

A Formal Feeling retells Oneal's childhood story about the figure skater, now cast as Anne Cameron, and the trumpeter, now Anne's father who has "traded in his trumpet for a professorship in medieval history . . . and plays riffs on Dante" ("Metamorphosis," 10). Anne wants to spin and twirl deliriously on a never-ending carousel ride alone with her father, like her predecessor the world-famous skater who whirls to the spirited music of the trumpeter. Oneal once again captures every little girl's desire for an exclusionary relationship with her father. But, like Kate in *In Summer Light,* little girls grow up, and kingly fathers give way to princely young men. The dashing Mr. Cutting wins Kate's heart as Ian. This time Oneal brings the small island in the pond in her childhood back yard to full life as a real island, "a brightly colored place—Gauguin colors, Impressionist colors, a sensual landscape of light and flowers" ("Metamorphosis," 11). Unsuccessful at earning her father's focused attention, Kate looks to Ian to whisk her away, to be her trumpeter.

Can writers and readers, through fiction, finish unfinished business? With Kate, Oneal suggests it may not be finished, but it can be closed. After struggling all summer, Kate completes her paper about Prospero, seeing him finally as "morally, politically, humanly wrong" (*ISL,* 143) for ignoring his people's needs and using others selfishly and as "an old man . . . [whose] magic powers are nearly gone and then they are gone entirely" (*ISL,* 143). This passage metaphorically echoes Kate's own resolution with her father. Like every other child, Kate begins to see her parents as flawed and as weakened by the frailties inherent in being human. Anne Cameron can mourn her mother only when she accepts her as imperfect. Ultimately, children recognize that their parents have made decisions for intensely personal reasons, as Kate's mother has. All children lucky enough to outlive their parcnts must also see them as old, as Kate eventually sees her father. Refusal to acknowledge these inevitabilities threatens to trap children in their childhood, as Kate risks being trapped by her own limited, unforgiving vision of her parents. At the end of *In Summer Light,* Kate is not trapped; she looks back on the island she leaves, watching it float away, "fading into the middle distance as the ferry moved on" (*ISL,* 149). Awakening to a new understanding of her parents leads Kate to a new understanding of herself and allows her to move ahead, as Carrie, Anne, and all other children must move on to adulthood.

Oneal's three young adult novels return her not only to personal mythologies but also to ancient tales of awakening. While Oneal herself traces the classical roots embedded in *In Summer Light* (*HB,* 32–33), all three young adult novels summon elements of this mythic pattern. In *The Language of Goldfish,* Carrie wants to remain on her island of childhood, surrounded by the moat in which goldfish swim. She holds the key to unlock the childlike language of goldfish; she also has the power to leave the island. Yet Carrie is fearful of stepping into the world of adults. Her developing body frightens her. Sexual awakenings frighten her; she fears the kiss of a prince. In a variation on the mythic pattern of the 100-year sleep, Carrie invokes endless sleep in a suicide attempt, an attempt to prolong her idealized childhood. Dressed in a scratchy new jacket, 13-year-old Daniel Spangler may not be Carrie's knight in shining armor, but he does offer her genuine friendship, which helps her bridge childhood and adolescence. Anne Cameron seems encased in a crystal coffin of ice, similar to the glass coffin in which the choked Snow White was placed. Emotionally choked, cold, and distant, Anne seeks the solitariness of a patch of ice. On this metaphoric island, Anne, like Carrie, refuses to grow up. While Anne enjoys a young prince's company during the summer, it is her fall and ankle sprain that mandate rest. During this imposed passivity, Anne's sleep provides perspective on her childhood, on her mother and their relationship. Her waking is also an awakening. And Kate's story, a modern Sleeping Beauty:

Once upon a time on an island off the coast of Massachusetts there lived a famous painter and his wife. Now to this couple was born a daughter, and they named her Kate. All went well with them for a time, but then came the year that Kate was seventeen, and she fell into a curious state of lethargy. She began to languish there on the island, hedged all around by the thorny tangle of childhood memories. It was not from a jealous fairy's spell that Kate suffered. Rather it was from a thoroughly modern malady called mononucleosis, but the symptoms were much the same. Drowsy, dozing, full of lassitude, Kate rested, deep among the thorns and brambles of the family thicket. In time, of course, a prince arrived. He came riding one day to the place where Kate slept, not on a fine and spirited palfrey but in a car with broken-down springs. A graduate student from California, this prince had neither wealth nor title, yet he succeeded in awakening Kate. (*HB*, 33)

These three heroines—Carrie, Anne, and Kate—emerge from their modern adventures as strong and resilient young women, awakened to new possibilities of human connectedness.

7. Shaping and Refining

> Painting has to do with knocking yourself out day after day trying to get what you want to down on the canvas. Maybe it works and maybe it doesn't, but every day you try. That's what painting is. (*ISL*, 146)

After seeing her father painting and beginning to paint again herself, Kate Brewer passionately articulates the hard work of painting. Zibby Oneal might well have written these words about writing: it is hard work. The canvas has become a blank sheet of paper, the paintbrush is now a pen, the landscape a setting, the figures characters, and the subject a story to be told.

Oneal once recalled seeing Virginia Woolf's manuscripts for *Orlando* and remembered being fascinated at the kinds of changes someone like Woolf, "someone so precise about language," would make. A similar curiosity impelled us to contact the Kerlan Collection in Minnesota about Oneal's manuscripts. They graciously made available copies of the three young adult novels in progress: two drafts of *The Language of Goldfish,* three drafts of *A Formal Feeling,* and five drafts of *In Summer Light*. What secrets might these earlier versions hold?

One might expect to see mostly word changes as Oneal tightened her use of language and strengthened her images. The manuscripts, however, revealed more substantive changes. The best of Oneal's writing is poetic and lyrical. The manuscripts suggest that this talent, this facility with words, yields vivid, evocative images early on. Metaphors and similes often remain unchanged from the first draft of a novel to the published version. Through four drafts, Ian offers Kate "a bouquet of forks" (*ISL,* 27); through two versions, Carrie imagines "silly pink bouquets, curling up, shriveling, dropping off like leaves" in the pattern of her wallpaper (*LG,* 7); and for three drafts, Anne worries about going home for the holidays because "whole pieces of what had once been real would vanish like snowflakes melting . . . leaving nothing" (*FF,* 85). In the final version, Oneal adds "but a memory of perfection" (*FF,* 85) to this last image. While the integrity of the image remains intact, a subtle change intensifies it and tightly connects it to the novel's thematic concerns. Perhaps because similes are marked by the words *like* or *as,* they are more obvious and therefore potentially intrusive. Many of Oneal's similes work well to aid readers in envisioning the scene. However, it is in her use of metaphor that Oneal's talent as a writer impresses. This sentence from *A Formal Feeling* uses both simile and metaphor: "Cascades of ivory and silver notes spilled onto the rug around her like brilliant rain" (116). The metaphor of music's being so magnificent that it fills to the point of spilling and cascading onto the rug, out of the piano, consuming the entire room, succeeds in capturing the majesty of the music being played. Conversely, the simile "like brilliant rain" shifts the image from an auditory one to a visual one. In this case, the simile threatens to weaken the power of the metaphor.

In reading Oneal's holographs and manuscripts, one is also privy to her editor's comments. Deborah Brodie, Oneal's editor at Viking Press, applauds the artistry of Oneal's language and descriptions. Responding to *In Summer Light* Brodie writes, "The peach-colored cat is the first of many, many descriptions that are startling, vivid, soothing, exciting or that evoke curiosity and a new way of looking. To single out the ones I love would mean recopying almost the entire manuscript!"[1] In letters and on tags scattered throughout the holographs and typewritten manuscripts, Brodie provides positive feedback and calls for clarification or development. The intimacy of their collaboration extends beyond the exchange of manuscripts and correspondence. They meet, talk on the telephone, and work independently to direct the manuscript into its final form.

In a discussion of their unique author-editor relationship, Oneal and Brodie reveal their shared belief that an editor is far more than one who corrects punctuation:

> "The first stages are the hardest for Zibby," says Brodie. "Some authors write at white heat and then revise in great pain, whereas I think she painfully gets something down and then . . ."
>
> "Revising, that's a cakewalk," interjects Oneal.
>
> "You work hard at it," Brodie insists.
>
> "Well, but by then I know where I'm going," replied Oneal. "To me, what's hard is the time I wonder where on earth I'm going, if anywhere! But Deborah's very good to work with on revisions, because she's so meticulous. It would kill me to have somebody go through it in a slapdash way . . . I want that very detailed sort of editing, because that means we're really communicating about the character and the situation. That's how I write and that's how I want to be edited." (Smith, 97–98)

This exchange evidences the very nature of the collaboration between Oneal and Brodie: clarifying and building on ideas. The editor gives the manuscript close, careful readings. Her job is not to rewrite the story but to guide the author to the best version of that story.

The evolution of story involves both major and minor modifications. In reading manuscripts of Oneal's three young adult novels, we focused on the changes that intrigued us and made a substantial impact on the published novel. (Of course, Oneal may have made alterations to the manuscripts in conversations with Brodie; our observations are limited by the manuscripts and written correspondence.)

Two significant deletions strengthen the final version of *The Language of Goldfish*. The first occurs at the outset of the novel. En route to Dr. Ross's office, Carrie encounters a disturbing old woman in a meeting that reminds Carrie of one of her first visits to Dr. Ross when she had seen the same woman. Now, nearly a year later, seeing her again touches off a chain of emotions in Carrie: feelings of identification with the crazy woman, doubts about her own sanity, and fright about herself and about the possible danger the woman posed. This scene attempts to foreshadow Carrie's growing instability. The self-reflection effectively builds Carrie's character, but the old woman seems superfluous. In a novel so tightly bound to Carrie's inner thoughts, tensions, and anxieties, the woman inappropriately externalizes Carrie's personal insanity.

Oneal also eliminates a second scene that originally fell near the novel's conclusion. After intentionally breaking a lamp because she has learned of Mrs. Ramsay's plans to leave with a man, Carrie journeys to her old neighborhood. Her visit includes the family's old apartment and her best friend Tanya's now-razed apartment. Oneal's descriptions are characteristically detailed and sensual, conveying a strong sense of place and of Carrie's childhood activities. Carrie is acutely and obviously cognizant of the changes in her neighborhood. This awareness leads to her conscious statement about the changes that have occurred within her as she has grown out of childhood. Indeed, the scene concludes with Carrie's return home, where she tells her sister about the onset of her period. From beginning to end, melodrama undermines the scene. Carrie's reaction to her recognition of Mrs. Ramsay as a whole person, not just her friend or her teacher, stays in character. Her distress at Mrs. Ramsay's sexuality fits Carrie's fear of growing up. Carrie's return to her old home, however, seems forced and pedantic. She need not revisit childhood in order to bid it farewell. If anything, deleting the scene reinforces the thematic power of the novel because Carrie must move ahead without first moving back. Marking Carrie's coming of age with menstrual blood lacks the subtlety that distinguishes Oneal's final manuscript.

Even a single word change affects the integration of character and theme. In the conclusion of *The Language of Goldfish,* the first and second drafts have Carrie seeing the island for the last time. The published book reads: "And that was when she saw the island" (*LG,* 178). The deletion of the word *last* heightens the potency of Carrie's revelation, quietly conveying Carrie's first recognition of the island as the romanticization of her childhood. When Carrie simply sees the island, readers know that she sees it truly for the first and the last time, naming it "nothing more than a pile of rocks" (*LG,* 178). Seen nakedly and thus robbed of its power, the island can no longer haunt Carrie, and she can return it to the domain of childhood.

Similarly, the two earlier manuscripts of the novel conclude with Carrie's passing the island on to eight-year-old Sarah and running toward the lights of the Spanglers' and her house, a symbolic welcoming of her own adolescence. In the published novel, Carrie does not run; rather, "hugging her sweater around her, she turned and walked toward them" (*LG,* 179). Running suggests an exuberance and joie de vivre in adolescence foreign to Carrie's cautious, tentative nature. She may have acknowledged and even accepted the inevitability of change in her life, but she does not yet embrace it.

Three working drafts of *A Formal Feeling* preceded the published novel. The opening remains virtually unchanged, as does the narrative intention of the novel. Burdened by her mother's death, Anne hesitantly returns to her family home and her father's new wife during a school vacation. Page numbering from draft to draft dramatically reveals the kinds of changes made in the novel. For example, at one point in the middle of the book, what had been page 59 is followed immediately by page 154, then pages 155 and 156, followed by pages 27–36, then page 60. Oneal employs the cut-and-paste method to revise the order of completed, already written scenes. For the most part, scenes remain intact but are lifted in entirety and shifted in the novel.

Some scenes are changed slightly. In the original manuscript, Anne tries to contact her father or Spencer at home to pick her up after she falls skating. Unable to reach them, she telephones Dory. Anne's reliance on Dory at this point in the novel is not entirely believable; it happens too early and breaks with Anne's character. Anne's growth to that point in the novel has not included reaching out to Dory, even for help. In the second version,

Anne does not seek Dory's assistance. More believably, Anne hobbles home on her own, and it is Dory who comes to Anne's rescue. The reversal allows Anne to remain true to her character and, in demonstrating Dory's immediate and genuine care for Anne, develops Dory's character. Further, it provides additional reasons for Anne's eventual acceptance of Dory.

Occasionally a scene is completely eliminated. The first manuscript includes Anne's detailed recollection of her mother's dying at home. She remembers the medical paraphernalia, the nurses, and the disorder in the house created by her mother's illness. Omission of the scene heightens the contrast between Dory's clutter and Anne's mother's refined household order. Oneal intensifies Anne's sense of her mother's perfection by placing the process of dying outside the action of the novel. In addition, to extend Mrs. Cameron's illness at home would provide Anne with time and opportunity to resolve some of her feelings before her mother dies and would detract from the severity of Anne's current crisis.

A second important elimination stems from Mr. Cameron's suggestion in the first draft that Anne go to boarding school. The suggestion reveals his need to go beyond his wife's death and affirms his interest in a romantic relationship with Dory. Deleting the scene removes the responsibility of the suggestion from Mr. Cameron. He cannot dismiss his daughter so lightly. Further, to ground Anne's character, Oneal needs to retain Anne's sense of importance to her father. If she detects from him a desire to have her gone from his home and his life, the novel loses its powerful core. Anne would fight two battles then: loss of her mother and rejection by her father. Deletion of the scene further directs the novel toward Anne's conflict with her mother.

In the original manuscript, Anne's struggle centers on questioning her mother's love. By the second draft and in the published piece, Anne asks herself the more frighteningly truthful question: "Did I ever love my mother at all?" (*FF,* 155). Implying Anne's responsibility, the second question is more painful to ask and more difficult to answer. What happened? Why did the key question of the novel change? Perhaps one answer is that in writing the story for the first time, in finding its direction and listening to its characters, Oneal uncovered the real question.

Uncovering is the essence of the changes from the second to the third drafts. In the second draft, Spencer tries to explain to Anne his feelings about his mother's death, and, by way of supporting the difficulty she experiences, he shares with her ways in which he coped. Oneal drops this action. By the third draft, Spencer's coping precedes the opening of the novel, and Oneal can use him to elaborate on Anne's need to come to terms with her mother's death. Spencer's grieving remains outside the novel, and Anne's difficulty becomes more central.

Between the second and third drafts, Oneal remedies a tendency to say too much. Ridding the text of overt explanation and self-conscious analysis, the insights Oneal attributes to her characters gain strength. For example, in the second draft, having said that she and her mother "had loved each other in their imperfect ways" (*FF,* 156), Oneal elaborates on the implied meaning. The explanation is crossed out in the third and final draft; "and it was all right" (*FF,* 156) simply and directly follows the statement. The juxtaposition of these two thoughts reveals Anne's growth; not only can she recognize imperfections in her mother and in herself but also she can accept them. Further, Oneal's resistance to explaining what the text means opens it to readers to create their own meaning.

No major changes occur between the third, final draft and the published novel. Brodie's comments and Oneal's responses are scattered throughout this version. However, these modifications, along with some subtle word alterations, serve only to confirm the appropriateness of earlier changes and underscore the consistency of character.

In Summer Light had a curious beginning: Oneal sent it to Brodie as part of *A Formal Feeling*; Brodie separated them: "It was two books: one of them was about summer and heat and sweat and light, and the other had ice and cold and winter" (Smith, 97).

Looking at five drafts of *In Summer Light* presents a unique challenge. Correspondence between Brodie and Oneal addresses changes that do not correlate to any of the five manuscripts from the Kerlan Collection that define our examination. Also, our copies of the manuscripts are not dated. We ordered the manuscripts according to the sequence described in one of Brodie's letters.[2] In this discussion we will refer to the following progression of manuscript titles:

Version 1	The Studio: Morning
Version 2	Prospero's Island
Version 3	The Middle Distance
Version 4	Sea Change
Version 5	In Summer Light

To make an obvious observation, the title of the book metamorphosed as the novel evolved. The same experimentation with title does not seem to be the case with the two other novels. Exploration of a father-daughter relationship remains the one constant throughout all variations of *In Summer Light*. Marcus Brewer was created as an egotistical, arrogant, talented artist, and Kate stayed a gifted and embittered young woman who seeks her father's approval.

Except in this raw outline of narrative direction, the first version is dramatically different from the others. Secondary characters, such as Frances and Mrs. Hilmer, do not appear. Another family figures prominently in the thematic thrust of the novel as it parallels the often difficult parent–child relationship. References to *The Aeneid,* in which Aeneas carries his father out of burning Troy, play a significant role. Ian, in this version named Ethan, represents the burden parents present to their children. So many other permutations of the father-daughter conflict reduce, for the reader, the conflict between Kate and her father. The enormity of the tension as it pertains specifically to Kate has less emotional impact if readers must examine it in situations apart from Kate's.

"The Studio: Morning" includes some melodrama atypical of Oneal's writing and certainly out of character for Kate Brewer. In reevaluating her relationship with her father, Kate discovers her own deeply felt anger at him. Unlike the final portrayal of Kate, here she does not channel her anger; rather, she grasps a poker and thinks about attacking the painting her father made of her as a 10-year-old. In true chivalric fashion, Ethan (Ian) stops her destruction and listens to Kate vent years of anger toward her father.

A scene, just as sensational, immediately follows this one. Kate receives a telephone call in the middle of the night in which she learns that her father has had a heart attack. Kate's weeping leads to an unrealistic hospital scene in which Kate and her father review their past together and openly make advances toward a new understanding and acceptance of each other. This version concludes with a discussion of art and techniques. Marcus becomes her teacher; Kate becomes his pupil. It ends with Kate's memory of a fledgling bird just discovering its wings and learning to fly on its own.

These two scenes stretch the credibility of our understanding of Marcus Brewer. The father Kate remembers with such ambivalence, the self-immersed father who paints a study of light in which his daughter is not the subject but is merely an object, defies sudden transformation into a caring protector. It may be a happy ending but not a realistic one.

Between versions 1 and 2, Oneal begins to strip the sentimentality that plagues them. In the first manuscript, Kate unabashedly states her love to Ethan (Ian). At Brodie's suggestion, Oneal subdues that declaration. Kate asks Ethan (Ian) to take her to Boston. The words may change, but Kate's—and Ethan's (Ian's)—feelings do not. However, the statement has gained a subtlety and shyness consistent with Kate's first experience of love. It has lost an edge of confidence and defiance inconsistent with Kate's character.

In "Prospero's Island," Leah appears for the first time. As a careful listener and good friend, Leah becomes an important agent of Kate's growth. The ways in which Leah supports Kate change somewhat from version to version; however, Leah's primary function does not.

Even the title of this manuscript suggests its many references to Shakespeare's *The Tempest*. Brodie points out the need to lessen this emphasis in one of her letters. By the third draft, the play works as metaphor for Kate's epiphany about her father rather than as a conscious attempt to rewrite *The Tempest* in a contemporary setting.

In version 2, Kate returns to the island during the summer to recuperate, while in earlier ones she returned to her annual summer work as a mother's helper. Eliminating this role simultaneously rids the novel of an extraneous plot. The Johnson family is no longer necessary as Kate's employer and leaves the manuscript. The father-daughter relationship is then connected more tightly and more exclusively to Kate. Furthermore, Kate's illness, her confinement, and her frustration allow her to be "a pain in the ass sometimes, and that's good; she's sensitive but not wimpy" (Brodie, 1984).

From the second to the third manuscript, Oneal decreases overt sentimentality still further. In the first two versions, Kate affectionately calls her father "Papa." As Oneal explores the father-daughter relationship, Kate perceives him as less and less affectionate. He grows into himself as Marcus Brewer, genius and egocentric painter, and out of the loving role as Papa. In addition, in the first manuscript, Kate does not create a prize-winning painting but experiments with watercolors, attempting to imitate impressionistic technique and apply instruction from her father; in the second, she does paint the meadow and wins a prize for it when she is 12; by the third draft, Kate wins the blue ribbon for a painting done during her freshman year in high school. By increasing her age, Oneal endows Kate with the seriousness of a painter whom Marcus Brewer perceives as a tangible threat. Also in the second, but not third, version, Kate discusses her portrait of Frances with her father. The discussion centers around Kate's need to include figures and his preference for abstractions rather than objects or people. This scene articulates Kate's unique vision as an artist and also distinguishes it from Marcus Brewer's. However, Oneal more subtly and more effectively accomplishes these goals by deleting this scene from the published book. Throughout, she invests Kate with the qualities necessary to make this discovery about herself and her art. In the book, Kate, with the reader, finds her way on her own; comparisons with her father are submerged and internal rather than protracted and obvious.

In "The Middle Distance," version 3, there are minor changes, such as Ethan to Ian, which do not dramatically alter the focus of the novel. Reliance on *The Tempest* continues to disappear. Also in this version, Kate discusses with her mother her art, her philosophy of the purpose and place of art, and her intention to break from her father's tradition. Such a straightforward dialogue stiffens Kate's character; she intellectualizes what she feels too much rather than simply feeling it, as she does in the final version. Yet Kate's relationship with her mother does deepen in this version, an alteration that profoundly influences the published novel. In the two earlier versions, Kate knows undeniably that her first set of paints is a gift from her mother. In the third version, Kate consistently believes that the paints are from her father, and she interprets this as his encouragement of her talent. When, in the third version and in the final book, Kate realizes the paints were from her mother, their relationship crystallizes in a new way. Her father remains as unseeing as he has always been, and Kate perceives the extent of her mother's support and love. She becomes less critical of her mother and for the first time begins to see the truth of her mother's contentment: she is honestly happy with her life. Kate can then release her mother from the confines of her assessment of who Floss Brewer should be and accept her as mother, supporter, and friend. In addition, it is important to the final book that Kate think her father gave her the paints. In order to contrast her adolescent dissatisfaction with his lack of attention, Kate needs to have felt that he did know her and did nurture her talent at one time. If she does not hold this belief, their conflict is less abrasive.

By the fourth version, "A Sea Change," Oneal has written the story she wants to tell. Theme, characters, setting, and scenes are fully realized here. The only notable changes stem from Oneal's deletion of excess explanation. For example, after Kate paints the rock with red clay, she ruminates on her feeling of contentment. In evocative prose, Oneal has already shown this contentment. Telling the reader of Kate's pleasure reduces the impact of the passage and muddies it with redundancy.

Not surprisingly, the fifth version, "In Summer Light," closely resembles the published book. Brodie's comments on early drafts were usually in substantial letters reacting to an overall view of the book and asking Oneal to consider changes, expansions, and deletions growing out of Brodie's idea of the novel's cohesion. In this version, hardly a page fails to earn a quick, brief, and supportive comment from Brodie. "Good," "great," and "wonderful" fill the margins of the manuscript. Such positive response must encourage Oneal to make the few minor changes necessary, primarily deletions that overstate.

A review of these manuscripts reveals much about Oneal's process and concerns as a writer. On many occasions it seems that Oneal feels protective of her characters. In an early version of *The Language of Goldfish*, Mrs. Ramsay calls Carrie to tell her that she has won a prize in an art contest. In one draft of *A Formal Feeling*, Anne goes to a New Year's Eve party with Eric, and they rekindle their summer romance. And in an early version of *In Summer Light*, Kate and Marcus Brewer reconcile. Oneal seems to want to give these characters happy endings; however, she has created realistic worlds in which people compromise and adapt but do not change over the course of a sentence. In refining the novels, she comes to see her characters as people with real limitations, which often preclude fairy-tale endings. Marcus could not reconcile with Kate, but Kate can gain self-knowledge, which allows her a new vision and ultimate acceptance of her father. Anne works hard enough to place one important relationship in perspective; others will come later. And Carrie will continue to paint and continue to heal even without winning the art prize. To win it would be unnecessary and sentimental.

Oneal's finished versions include greater uncertainty and ambiguity than earlier ones. She may begin the books out of an underlying need to work through and put closure on unfinished business, but she courageously pursues, defines, and sharpens her characters. They become so believable, so real that they too have unfinished business. Oneal's true gifts are the bravery to put aside herself and the vision to allow her characters their own selfhood. In offering readers profound insight into themselves through her characters, Oneal sees the awakening potential of unfinished business.

8. Letting the Outside In

In talking with Zibby Oneal, we came to see a personal side of the author: as daughter, sister, wife, and mother, as well as writer. She shared treasured memories of childhood and discussed her aspirations in writing. In examining each novel, we looked at the literary integrity of Oneal's vision and considered the novels from their thematic and aesthetic foundations. We addressed the central theme of awakening as Oneal incorporates it into the fabric of each story. And in moving to a consideration of the novels in progress, we looked at the hard work of rewriting—of perfecting an image, a word, an idea. It is this aspect of writing that Oneal finds the most challenging and the most rewarding. So far, we have concentrated solely on Oneal and her work. Other opinions and attitudes have not distracted us from this immersion. However, like Anne Cameron, we now need to break out of this crystal shell and allow the noise of the outside world to enter. Oneal speaks to this necessity: "The movement away and out into the world, into concern for other people, has to happen: you aren't an adult until you make that move" (Smith, 98).

Oneal entered the world of young adult literature at the height of popularity of the problem novel. At first glance, *The Language of Goldfish* seems a logical addition to this tradition. The duality of insanity and suicide integral to the novel's plot intrigues would-be readers with the expectation of sensational subject matter. "But it would be a mistake to include this novel in the wave of pop-sociological fiction about teenage trauma. . . . No doubt many young readers will be drawn to the story because it promises to show 'what it's like to go crazy' . . . but most readers will see a good deal of themselves in Carrie."[1] It is precisely that recognition that raises this novel above the mundane. Readers see in Carrie's struggle their own difficult trials of becoming. Like Carrie, they too are "neither friends nor angels, just real people doing their flawed best in a flawed world."[2]

Further critical appraisal addresses various aspects of the novel that support character and deepen the reading experience. In addition to receiving starred reviews in the influential periodicals *Booklist* and *School Library Journal* and an enthusiastic review in the *Horn Book Magazine, The Language of Goldfish* earned honor throughout the children's book world. The American Library Association named it a "Best Book for Young Adults" and listed it as a "Notable Book" of 1980 and as one of the "Best of the Best Books, 1970–1982." The title was included on *School Library Journal*'s "Best Books of the Year" list and was named a "Reviewers' Choice" and a "Contemporary Classic" by *Booklist*. Individual reviewers comment on the technical strengths of the novel, from convincing dialogue to evocative imagery to controlled use of metaphor to "language that is poetic and precise" (Milton, 65).

In a brief evaluation of Oneal's three young adult novels, M. Jean Greenlaw agrees to a great extent with these laudatory reviews of *The Language of Goldfish*. She finds the metaphor of the island ineffectual, however: "The use of rich metaphor in descriptive passages and short sentences in dialogue heightens the sensation of personal isolation within a vibrant world. The only device that doesn't work is the image of the island in the middle of the goldfish pond. It plays a central role as the metaphor for Carrie's anguish, yet the image keeps slipping and is not fully recognized."[3] This very slippage conveys the elusive nature of both reality and childhood. For Oneal to have described the island in detail would have robbed Carrie of her own recognition of the island, in both its physical and symbolic terms. The novel's conclusion reveals that knowing the island allows Carrie to leave it. She cannot clarify the ephemeral, even hazy, qualities of the island until the novel's ultimate resolution; to do so would undermine the novel's—and Carrie's—final epiphany. Indeed, Carrie's "search for the magic island, which she can see in her imagination but no longer recognize in reality, is a resonant metaphor for the lost illusions of childhood" (Milton, 65).

While inspired by and built around an Emily Dickinson poem, an overtly literary metaphor, *A Formal Feeling* appeals to young adult readers in part because of the drama inherent in the loss of a parent. The fear of this loss intensifies during adolescence when ambivalence complicates relationships with parents. Death denies the young adult a mature resolution to her ambiguous feelings: "It takes nerve in a novelist to construct a story which depends largely on the posthumous influence of an invisible character. |Here| the device works; we care about the outcome of retrospective disclosures because only the truth, complex and ambivalent, seems likely to set Anne free."[4]

As with *The Language of Goldfish,* Oneal successfully incorporates a recognizable adolescent issue into this fiction without letting it dominate. Both Carrie and Anne have problems, yet neither book is a "problem novel." Oneal walks the fine line between drama and melodrama masterfully: "Out of |the American children's book| background of therapeutic literature on how to deal with menstruation, sexuality, color prejudice, or alcoholism, |*A Formal Feeling*| is a book dealing with bereavement but offering something more."[5] Critics describe that "something more" in a variety of ways. Zena Sutherland speaks of Oneal's "perceptive meshing of personalities and relationships that are strongly drawn."[6] Also commenting on Oneal's skillful character portrayals, Stephanie Zvirin addresses the novel's pacing, "slow and deliberate," "scenes of great emotional intensity," and Oneal's "highly descriptive style . . . |which| captures Anne's conflicting feelings with subtlety and perception."[7] Initially dubious about the pacing, British critic Peter Hunt concludes that Oneal's stylistically "restrained approach" is not only appropriate to the novel but also complements its psychological reality.[8] Greenlaw writes about the consistency of Oneal's imagery in this novel and cites her "excellent use of detail [to create] suspense by using small incidents to build to the climax. This is a powerful novel that probes human emotions with insight and elegant style" (742). In contrast, Paul Heins finds that despite its controlled narrative, "the style—self-consciously descriptive and allusive—tends to be antiseptic. Centering on Anne's state of mind more than on her emotions, the novel not only lacks intensity but [also] fails to attain the power of effective understatement."[9] What appears to be negative in this statement in fact underscores the technical achievements of this novel. "Antiseptic" deftly captures Anne's character: she wants clean relationships, unsoiled by emotion; she leaves the sterilized air on the plane and expects to return to the same sanitary house her mother kept. Indeed, the novel's central intensity stem from Anne's acute denial of her emotions. She "freezes" her emotions. Formality characterizes Anne's state of mind; she analyzes and intellectualizes, but she does not feel. The primary motifs of the novel—cold, ice, blue, and distance—provide the symbolic language that underpins—and understates—its thematic essence.

A Formal Feeling also received public and literary recognition. In addition to starred reviews in *Booklist* and *School Library Journal,* the American Library Association included it on its lists of "Notable Books," "Best Books for Young Adults," and "Best of the Best Books, 1970–1982." The *New York Times* named it a "Best Book of the Year," and *American Bookseller* cited it as a "Pick of the Lists." Like *The Language of Goldfish,* it was recommended by *Booklist* as a "Reviewer's Choice." Beyond this impressive praise, Oneal won her first major award for children's fiction with this novel: the Christopher Award, given annually to a book that combines artistic excellence, "the highest values of the human spirit," and popularity within its audience.

"With [a] powerful, evocative coming-of-age story [*In Summer Light*], Oneal tops her two previous [prize]-winners"[10] and adds one of the most coveted children's book awards to an already striking group of critical successes. The Boston Globe–Horn Book Award, presented annually since 1967, was given to Oneal for *In*

Summer Light in the category of "Outstanding Fiction" in 1986.
Not surprisingly, the American Library Association promoted this
novel on its lists of "Notable Books" and "Best Books for Young
Adults."

Complementing starred reviews (in the *Horn Book* and *School
Library Journal*) critics widely praised this book. Trevelyn
Jones's review typifies the novel's public reception: "It's hard to
say which is more impressive in this literate, complex story—
Oneal's use of language, imagery and color, or the development of
her finely drawn characters."[11] This set of reviews evaluates in
glowing terms the aspects of Oneal's fiction that reviews of her
earlier novels also acknowledge: controlled, graceful imagery;
deft character portrayals; and elegant style. Perhaps because art
plays a central role in this novel and Oneal adheres closely to
seeing and describing through Kate's artistic eyes, reviewers comment extensively on the author's painterly style. They note her
talent in capturing visual images in words and her ability to in-
fuse the novel with light and color.

Unlike reviews of the two earlier young adult novels, this particular group also measures Oneal's growth and maturity as a
writer. A collage of such comments addresses this increased
mastery:

> The literary resolution grows more polished and mature with
> each novel. . . . *In Summer Light* is also her most ambitious
> and coherent work to date.[12]

> The novel surpasses her multiple prize winners.[13]

> A coming-of-age novel that is light-years above most others.
> (Jones, 186)

> For those YA readers who have acquired a taste for quiet elo-
> quently written books that explore complex human experiences
> of the mind and heart, *In Summer Light* will be a special lit-
> erary treat of sustaining nourishment and illumination. Like
> Willa Cather, Ms. Oneal is an author whose clear, vivid writ-
> ing style transcends age categories and other classification
> boundaries.[14]

Across the three young adult novels, reviewers largely characterize Oneal's work as accomplished literary experiences for perceptive, insightful readers. The novels appeal to readers who identify with an intelligent, thoughtful heroine whose story is largely introspective. Plot remains secondary; action is interior. Despite the distance expected from a third-person narration, Oneal establishes an unusual and remarkable intimacy between reader and character. Readers watch Carrie's journey toward stability even as they empathize with her psychological struggle. Readers are both observers and participants in this story. Oneal sustains this subjective focus through the use of objective images. For example, in *The Language of Goldfish,* she describes the familiar experience of looking through a kaleidoscope, seeing the fluid yet jagged changes:

> "It seemed as though things suddenly slipped sideways," she said. "Inside my head colors—queer colored shapes—began to tumble around like the colored glass in a kaleidoscope. There was a kind of roaring noise. My head began to float. I thought I was sick. I thought I was going to faint."
>
> "I held onto the door frame and shut my eyes. Behind my eyes I saw the colors all beautiful and tumbling." (*LG,* 12)

This concrete image enables readers to imagine wholly Carrie's experience, to be inside Carrie's mind and feel what she feels.

Certainly these sensitive, intelligent, reflective heroines are not alone in the contemporary world of young adult fictional characters. Veteran authors like Paula Fox and newcomers such as Jenny Davis also create characters whose intense, interior, emotional lives form the substance of stories. Even with this company, the quiet, introspective novel remains distinctive and atypical in today's young adult fiction. Louder, action-oriented titles represent a larger portion of the market. Authors like Robert Cormier, S. E. Hinton, and Walter Dean Myers write compelling narratives in which the adolescent protagonists face challenges originating in the outside world. Initially it is the school situation in Cormier's *The Chocolate War* that promotes Jerry Renault's character development. Gangs and violence dominate Ponyboy Curtis's story. In *Fallen Angels,* Richie Perry enlists in the army to escape home, only to find himself in the front line of the Vietnam War. Conversely, Oneal fights the battles of heart and mind. Her characters resolve issues of personal relationships in an ostensibly narrower framework. Their struggles may seem less dramatic, less glorious, less important than these others. However, all young adult fiction strives to answer the fundamental questions of adolescence: Who am I? Where do I fit in? What will I become? Some authors place these issues of identity in a societal, even global, context. Others, like Zibby Oneal, address them unpretentiously at home.

Notes and References

Preface

1. Zibby Oneal, "In Summer Light," *Horn Book,* January–February 1987, 34; hereafter cited in text as *HB*.
2. Wendy Smith, "Working Together," *Publishers Weekly,* 21 February 1986, 97; hereafter cited in text.

2. Charting a Course

1. Zibby Oneal, *In Summer Light* (New York: Viking Press, 1985), jacket cover; hereafter cited in text as *ISL*.
2. Zibby Oneal, *War Work* (New York: Viking Press, 1971), 144; hereafter cited in text as *WW*.
3. Zibby Oneal, *Turtle and Snail* (Philadelphia: Lippincott, 1979), 9; hereafter cited in text as *TS*.
4. Zibby Oneal, *Grandma Moses: Painter of Rural America* (New York: Viking Press, 1986), 58; hereafter cited in text as *GM*.
5. Zibby Oneal, *A Long Way to Go* (New York: Viking Press, 1990), jacket copy; hereafter cited in text as *LW*.

3. Learning the Language

1. Zibby Oneal, *The Language of Goldfish* (New York: Viking Press, 1980), 8; hereafter cited in text as *LG*.
2. J. D. Salinger, *The Catcher in the Rye* (1951; New York: Bantam, 1981), 1.

4. Shattering Formality

1. Emily Dickinson, "After Great Pain," in *Complete Poems of Emily Dickinson,* ed. Thomas H. Johnson (Boston: Little, Brown, 1929).

2. Jane Donahue Eberwein, *Dickinson: Strategies of Limitation* (Amherst: University of Massachusetts Press, 1985), 141; hereafter cited in text.

3. Shakespeare, *The Tempest,* 5.1.7.

4. Zibby Oneal, *A Formal Feeling* (New York: Viking Press, 1982), 122; hereafter cited in text as *FF.*

5. William R. Sherwood, *Circumference and Circumstance: Stages in the Mind and Art of Emily Dickinson* (New York: Columbia University Press, 1968), 112–13.

6. Awakenings

1. Zibby Oneal, "Metamorphosis," unpublished manuscript of talk delivered at the Center for the Study of Children's Literature, Simmons College, Boston, 16 July 1987, 7; hereafter cited in text.

7. Shaping and Refining

1. Deborah Brodie to Zibby Oneal, 25 October 1984, Kerlan Collection, University of Minnesota, Minneapolis.

2. Ibid., 26 February 1985, Kerlan Collection.

8. Letting the Outside In

1. Joyce Milton, *New York Times Book Review,* 27 April 1980, 52.

2. Loralee MacPike, *Best Sellers,* April 1980, 39.

3. M. Jean Greenlaw, "Zibby Oneal," in *Twentieth Century Children's Writers,* ed. Tracy Chevalier and D. L. Kirkpatrick (Chicago and London: St. James Press, 1989), 742; hereafter cited in text.

4. Marion Glastonbury, "Missing Persons," *Times Educational Supplement,* 3 June 1983, 41.

5. Dorothy Nimmo, *School Librarian,* September 1983, 272.

6. Zena Sutherland, *Bulletin of the Center for Children's Books,* October 1982, 34.

7. Stephanie Zvirin, *Booklist,* 1 October 1982, 199.

8. Peter Hunt, *Signal Review of Children's Books 2,* 1984, 43.

9. Paul Heins, *Horn Book,* April 1983, 73–74.

10. *Kirkus Reviews,* 1 September 1985, 914–15.

11. Trevelyn Jones, *School Library Journal,* October 1985, 186.

12. Michele Landsberg, *New York Times Book Review,* 24 November 1985, 121.

13. *Publishers Weekly,* 2 August 1985, 69.

14. Leigh Dean, *Children's Book Review Service,* November 1985, 33.

Selected Bibliography

Primary Works

Picture Books

Maude and Walter. Illustrated by Maxie Chambliss. New York: Lippincott, 1985.
Turtle and Snail. Illustrated by Margot Tomes. Philadelphia: Lippincott,
1979.

Novels

A Formal Feeling. New York: Viking Press, 1982; Ballantine Books, 1983.
The Improbable Adventures of Marvelous O'Hara Soapstone. Illustrated
by Paul Galdone. New York: Viking Press, 1972.
In Summer Light. New York: Viking, 1985; Bantam, 1986.
The Language of Goldfish. New York: Viking, 1980; Ballantine, 1981.
War Work. Illustrated by George Porter. New York: Viking Press, 1971.

Other

Grandma Moses: Painter of Rural America. Illustrated by Donna Ruff.
New York: Viking Press, 1986.
A Long Way to Go. Illustrated by Michael Dooling. New York: Viking
Press, 1990.

Speeches

Acceptance speech for the 1986 Boston Globe–Horn Book Award for *In
Summer Light, Horn Book Magazine,* January/February 1987, 30–
33.

"Metamorphosis." Unpublished manuscript of talk delivered at the Center for the Study of Children's Literature, Simmons College, Boston, 16 July 1987.

Secondary Sources

Parts of Books

Chevalier, Tracy, and D. L. Kirkpatrick, eds. "Zibby Oneal." In *Twentieth-Century Children's Writers*. 3d ed. Chicago and London: St. James Press, 1989.

Commire, Anne, ed. "Zibby Oneal." In *Something about the Author*, 30:166–67. Detroit: Gale Research Company, 1983.

Locher, Frances C., Martha G. Conway, B. Hal May, and David Versical, eds. "Zibby Oneal." In *Contemporary Authors,* 106:381–82. Detroit: Gale Research Company, 1982.

Senick, Gerald J., and Melissa Reiff Hug, eds. "Zibby Oneal." In *Children's Literature Review,* 13:153–60. Detroit: Gale Research Company, 1987.

Stine, Jean C., and Daniel G. Marowski, eds. "Zibby Oneal." In *Contemporary Literary Criticism*, 30:279–81. Detroit: Gale Research Company, 1984.

Articles

Glastonbury, Marion. "Missing Persons." *Times Educational Supplement*, 3 June 1983, 41.

Kelso, Dorothy H. "Stories: Hard Fact and Deft Fantasy." *Christian Science Monitor,* 8 November 1972, 84.

McHargue, Georgess. "Coming of Age." *New York Times Book Review,* 14 November 1982, 48.

Smith, Wendy. "Working Together." *Publishers Weekly,* 21 February 1986, 97–98.

Letters

Brodie, Deborah. Letter to Zibby Oneal. 25 October 1984. Kerlan Collection, University of Minnesota, Minneapolis.

———. Letter to Zibby Oneal. 26 February 1985. Kerlan Collection, University of Minnesota, Minneapolis.

Selected Reviews

A Formal Feeling

Bowden, Laurie. *School Library Journal,* October 1982, 163.
Fisher, Margery. *Growing Point,* July 1983, 4102.
Heins, Paul. *Horn Book,* April 1983, 173–74.
Hunt, Peter. *Signal Review of Children's Books 2,* 1984, 43.
Nimmo, Dorothy. *School Librarian,* September 1983, 272.
Small, Robert C. *ALAN Review,* Winter 1983, 23.
Sutherland, Zena. *Bulletin of the Center for Children's Books,* October 1982, 34.
Zvirin, Stephanie. *Booklist.* 1 October 1982, 199.

Grandma Moses: Painter of Rural America

Hearne, Betsy. *Bulletin of the Center for Children's Books,* October 1986, 34.
Kewish, Nancy. *School Library Journal.* October 1986, 180.

The Improbable Adventures of Marvelous O'Hara Soapstone

Kirkus Reviews, 1 October 1972.

In Summer Light

Bulletin of the Center for Children's Books, October 1985, 34.
Dean, Leigh. *Children's Book Review Service,* November 1985, 33.
Jones, Trevelyn. *School Library Journal,* October 1985, 186.
Kirkus Reviews, 1 September 1985, 914–15.
Landsberg, Michele. *New York Times Book Review,* 24 November 1985, 21.
Publishers Weekly, 2 August 1985, 69.
Twitchell, Ethel R. *Horn Book,* November–December 1985, 742.
Zvirin, Stephanie. *Booklist,* 15 October 1985, 330.

The Language of Goldfish

Duncan, Jean. *English Journal,* April 1981, 77.
McDonnell, Christine. *Horn Book,* August 1980, 416.
MacPike, Loralee. *Bestsellers,* April 1980, 39.
Milton, Joyce. *New York Times Book Review,* 27 April 1980, 52, 65.
Pearl, Patricia. *Voice of Youth Advocates,* August 1980, 35.
Silver, Linda R. *School Library Journal,* February 1980, 709.

A Long Way to Go

Vasilakis, Nancy. *Horn Book,* July–August 1990, 457–58.

Maude and Walter
Kirkus Reviews, 15 December 1985, 1398.
Palmer, Nancy. *School Library Journal,* December 1985, 110.
Publishers Weekly, 16 August 1985, 70.
Showstack, Margo. *Children's Book Review Service,* January 1986, 49.

Turtle and Snail
Christolon, Blair. *School Library Journal,* November 1979, 68.
Publishers Weekly, 28 May 1979, 57.

War Work
Dishnica, Ronna. *School Library Journal,* April 1972, 138.
Sutherland, Zena. *Bulletin of the Center for Children's Books,* January
    1972, 77.

Index

Key:
A Formal Feeling = FF
The Improbable Adventures of Marvelous O'Hara Soapstone = IA
In Summer Light = ISL
The Language of Goldfish = LG
A Long Way to Go = LWG
Maude and Walter = MW
Turtle and Snail = TS
War Work = WW

The Authors

Susan P. Bloom is an assistant professor and director of the Center for the Study of Children's Literature at Simmons College. A former teacher at Newton High School, Brookline High School, Wellesley High School, and Palfrey Street School, she has long been involved in enriching the literary experience of young people. First as an instructor of freshman writing and then of a survey course in children's literature, Ms. Bloom has extended the connections between reading and writing. She makes regular contributions to a monthly "BookViews" column on new books for children and young adults in *The Boston Parents' Paper*. She wrote an article about the work of Paul Fleischman for *Twentieth Century Writers for Children*.

Cathryn M. Mercier is an assistant professor and associate director of the Center for the Study of Children's Literature at Simmons College. She reviews children's and young adult books for *The Five Owls* and writes for *The Boston Parents' Paper*. She contributed comprehensive pieces on Helen V. Griffith and on Beverly Cleary to *Twentieth Century Writers for Children* and an interview with Paula Fox in *Innocence and Experience: Essays and Conversations in Children's Literature*.

The Editor

Patricia J. Campbell has taught adolescent literature at UCLA and is the former assistant coordinator of young adult services at the Los Angeles Public Library. From 1978 to 1988 she reviewed young adult books in a monthly column for the *Wilson Library Bulletin,* for which she now writes a monthly review column on the independent press. Her five books include *Presenting Robert Cormier,* the first volume in Twayne's Young Adult Author Series. In 1989 she received the American Library Association Grolier Award for distinguished achievement with young people and books. She and her husband, David Shore, write and publish books on overseas campervan travel.